The Hidden Assembly Line

Gender Dynamics of Subcontracted Work in a Global Economy

Edited By Radhika Balakrishnan

Kumarian
Press, Inc.

The Hidden Assembly Line:
Gender Dynamics of Subcontracted Work
in a Global Economy

Published 2002 in the United States of America by Kumarian Press, Inc.,
1294 Blue Hills Avenue, Bloomfield, Connecticut 06002 USA

Production, design, indexing, and proofreading by City Desktop Productions, LLC.
The text of this book is set in Minion 10/13.

Printed in the USA on acid-free paper by Thomson-Shore, Inc.
Text printed with vegetable oil-based ink.

∞ The paper used in this publication meets the minimum requirements of the
American National Standard for Information Sciences—Permanence of Paper for
Printed Library Materials, ANSI Z39.48-1984.

Library of Congress Cataloging-in-Publication Data

The hidden assembly line : gender dynamics of subcontracted work in a global
economy / edited by Radhika Balakrishnan.
   p. cm.
Includes bibliographical references and index.
ISBN 1–56549–139–4 (pbk. : alk. paper)—ISBN 1–56549–140–8 (cloth : alk.
paper)
   1. Subcontracting—Asia—Case studies. 2. Women—employment—Asia—Case
Studies. 3. Home labor—Asia—Case Studies. 4. Globalization—Case Studies. I.
Balakrishnan, Radhika.

  HD2385.A77 H53 2001

338.4'76928'095—dc21

                2001038426

10 09 08 07 06 05 04 03 02   10 9 8 7 6 5 4 3 2 1

First Printing 2002

Contents

Acknowledgments

This book is a testament to the possibilities of collaboration and friendship over time and space. To Margaret Huang, my fellow traveler, conspirator, and friend I wish to express my deep gratitude for staying the course; this book is truly a shared accomplishment. The substance of this book would not have materialized if not for the dedication and commitment of the field research teams. Your advocacy on behalf of working women has inspired me and enriched my understanding of what is possible and necessary in the face of global economic forces. A very big thank you to Namrata Bali, Ratana Boonmathya, Lourdes Gula, Swarna Jayaweera, Saba Khattak, Rakwin Leechanavanichpan, Joseph Lim, Rosalinda Pineda Ofreneo, Yada Praparpun, Chandra Rodrigo, Najma Sadeque, Asad Sayeed, Thana Shanmugam, and Jeemol Unni.

I would also like to thank Lourdes Beneria for her inspiration, support, and scholarly assistance. This book is built upon the shoulders of her path-breaking work with Martha Roldan. Will Milberg was instrumental in opening my eyes to a growing body of work and provided incisive comments on early generations of this book.

The telling of the story would have no beginning if not for the women who were willing to share their lives. In spite of risks to their own precarious employment and their double and triple burdens, these women in Pakistan, Sri Lanka, Thailand, India, and the Philippines opened up their homes because they believed in what we were trying to accomplish.

Students at Marymount Manhattan College have served as a sounding board for my thinking. Their demands to make the work accessible and relevant have greatly shaped the language and structure of this book. I would also want to acknowledge the College's support of my work, expressed most concretely in awarding me a leave fellowship, just at the right time.

The Asia Foundation played an integral part in the making of the original research through its financial and institutional support. And I want to personally thank the staff that supported the research that inspired this book.

Josyln Barnes is a brilliant editor. Across countries and linguistic styles she helped bring coherence to the entire text (and on deadline!). I would also like to thank Vijay

K. Balakrishnan for his text review and substantive comments on my chapters. To Linda Beyus, editor at Kumarian Press, who believed in the promise of this book before a word was written, I'd like to thank for her faith in this project and in me.

Many friends have earned awards for listening to me as I shaped ideas and got periodically "whiggy:" Itty Abraham, Diane Elson, Shelly Feldman, Shalmali Guttal, Leila Hessini, Mehlika Hoodbhoy, Nikki Jones, Hande Keklik, Uma Narayan, Anita Nayar, Antony Romero, Meenakshi Srinivasan, and Jyotsna Uppal. Special thanks to Anika Rahman whose eleventh hour heroics made this book possible.

To my mother and father, I wish to express my gratitude for embracing my adventures.

Lastly, I want to thank David Gillcrist for his undying support, editorial help, and who typed when my hands quit working; I never imagined friendship to be so sweet.

Introduction

Radhika Balakrishnan

There was a growing interest among the nongovernmental organizations (NGOs) working in Asia to better contextualize their labor organizing work within a global economic framework. Activists were finding that a purely localized organizing strategy could not keep pace with the effects of the constantly changing structures of global capital accumulations. The changes in production patterns, particularly those that employed flexible production techniques, were greatly affecting the ability of activists to organize at the local level. Since the 1970s, rather than an increase in mass assembly production, industrialization in Asia has been typified by a mixed system based on free trade zones, subcontracting firms, and sweatshops (Ong 1997, 61).

This book is the result of a collaborative process that sought to break new ground by changing the way that most research is conducted. I was asked a few years ago to develop a research project for the Asia Foundation for its Women's Economic and Legal Rights Program.[1] It is important to note at the outset that the contents of this book express the views of the contributors and do not claim to represent the views of the Asia Foundation. Though the initial research was done under the auspices of the Asia Foundation, this book analyzes the initial findings from several perspectives.

From the ground up, the research that shaped this book focused on subcontracted work as a method for capturing the links between changing labor dynamics in several industries and macroeconomic policy at the national and international levels. Through anecdotal evidence it became clear that women were the primary workers, particularly in small shops and home-based work. We limited our investigation to only those two categories of subcontracted workers. The surveys tried to ascertain the changes in household dynamics as a result of this work. One of the main agendas of the research was to help better inform activist strategies for policy change by focusing on the complex gender dynamics that affected small-shop and home-based subcontracted work.

We focused on subcontracted workers because of the growth in that sector, the increasing academic interest in the relationship between changing economic conditions and flexibilization of work, and lastly to make connections between the lives of women on the ground and the changes in national and international conditions.[2] Using the work of Beneria and Roldan on industrial homework in Mexico as a starting point, we explored "the connection between economic processes and the dynamics of social relations within the household (Beneria and Roldan 1987, 1)."

This book is an attempt to examine the relationship between macroeconomic changes over the last few decades and women working in the subcontracted sector. Each chapter tries to illustrate the particularities of its own national context in the hope that, in the end, we construct a multi-layered picture of this dynamic relationship. The change in the macroeconomic conditions has had a significant impact on the conditions of work for women and gender relations in the household. As Isabella Bakker (1999) points out:

> Neoliberal political economy contributes to a marked fluidity between the public and private spheres, or the sites of production and reproduction, in several ways. Increasing informalization in advanced urban economies reconfigures not only economic relations between men and women, but also the sites where marketized labor occurs (Sassen 1998). Homework and other forms of subcontracting of labor, for instance, are not gender neutral because it is mainly women who adopt homework as an income strategy, and because men and women adopt homework for very different reasons and under different circumstances.

Women workers are drawn into poorly paid subcontracted work due to changes in the wider economy and the household division of labor. It is clear that there is little hope of significant change in their long-term standard of living or their empowerment as workers (Feldman and Ferretti 1998, 11). The effect of this work on women's rights as workers, the impact it exerts on gender dynamics in the household, and how this kind of paid work affects the double burden women have in caring for their families and earning a wage are of critical importance.

Some of the issues of concern to us in doing this research are: has subcontracted work increased and under what condition/circumstances; what are the forces that influence its prevalence; who benefits from this changing production pattern within countries and across nations; and what is the impact of this kind wage labor on women's social status and gender relations?

SETTING THE STAGE: VISITS TO THE FIELD

In my early visits to Thailand, India, the Philippines, and Sri Lanka, I was struck by the different ways that economic changes affected women. Though the evidence I present in this chapter is anecdotal, I think it illustrates the complexity of the relationship between gender dynamics and the changes in the domestic and international economy. I had the opportunity to visit many work sites while organizing and designing the research project. Below I describe a few of the places I visited and the conversations I had with workers to provide texture to the issues we analyzed.

Diversifying the Risk

In Thailand we visited several small shops in Bangkok that produced garments.[3] The woman who managed the small shop told us that the workshop had expanded because the decrease in the value of the Thai bhat had made Thai workers much cheaper to hire than others. She also stated that many of the larger garment factories had closed and that production was now being contracted out to these small shops. She was aware that these clothes were to be exported to West Africa. Her business was thriving. The workers were paid at a piece-rate and most often worked ten to twelve hours a day. The shop was a tiny place with poor lighting and inadequate ventilation. The children of the workers played in the shop, sitting on top of sewing machines or on the pile of clothes being sewn. In this particular shop there were a few men who were also sewing side by side with the women. When I asked about their work, they informed me that they were all professional tailors who had lost their jobs because of the lack of demand for hand-tailored goods due to the competition and popularity of ready-made garments.

The workers knew the difference between the piece-rate they received and that of the woman who ran the shop. The shop manager, on the other hand, did not have any idea how much the person who brought her the work was getting paid or how much the clothes sold for in the retail market. Though we tried very hard to follow the sub-contracting chain, very few of the shop managers knew where the garments went after they left the shop. Their immediate contact was the person who brought the work to them. There was no guarantee of payment for work done. The clothes had to pass a quality control check performed by yet another set of actors along the subcontracting chain. The shop managers often did not get paid on time and sometimes not at all. Since there are no written contracts, and the relationships along the production chain are informal and in constant flux, holding anyone accountable for payment was very difficult.

One of the impacts of the economic crisis in Thailand was to increase the amount of work that small subcontracted shops received. There was really no relevant labor legislation at the time and organizing these workers was very difficult since their employment status was so incredibly precarious. Some of the people we spoke to stated that many of the companies that closed down their factories actually stayed in the country and continued to produce garments through subcontracting arrangements. Some of the work also moved out of the cities to rural areas. Though it is difficult to assess the extent to which the closing of factories represented a shift in production sites from visible large factories to these hidden assembly lines, it is nevertheless evidence of a corporate strategy to decrease production costs and keep the production process flexible.

Production costs and business risks that would have been borne by the owner of a large factory are now shared by, and diversified among, a large number of individual entrepreneurs who are linked together in a pyramid-shaped network consisting of "center" and "satellite" factories. The factory's profit margin, and hence chance for survival, decreases as one moves from the "center" to the "satellite" or from the upper to the lower levels of the pyramid (Hsuing 1996, 70).

The strategy of using subcontracted small shops decreased the vulnerability of corporations to the changes in the market. In some instances, the workers had been a part of the organized work force that must now work at a piece-rate. There were also many workers, however, who were new entrants to the labor force who could work in these places because they could bring their children with them.

Penetration of Capital

In Thailand we also visited a small village a few hours outside of Khon Kean. We were taken there by an NGO that worked with weavers to maintain their traditional weaving techniques and materials. The weavers had lost a great deal of their market and were unable to sell their products at a competitive price. The amount of labor required to weave cloth with natural dyes made their products too expensive for the local market and the lack of international contacts made the international market difficult to penetrate. Many of the weavers were starting to do subcontracted piece-rate work for the international market. We visited a group of women who were putting together plastic flowers. One of the women had a family member who knew someone in the plastic flower business and brought the work to them. In rural areas in general and in some of the urban centers, in most of the countries we visited, women who ran small shops or home-workers relied on family networks to get work. In all the places I visited, the person who brought the work to the small shops were men, and the people who ran these shops were women.

The woman we met ran a small shop in her backyard and all the workers were her neighbors. This was one of the rare instances where we were able to actually identify the retailer of the product. There was a price tag for a shop in the United States that sold plastic flowers. Each stem sold for $3.99 per stem in the United States (about 160 Thai Bhat at the time). The women got paid 1 bhat per stem. They worked long hours for a piece-rate. One of the women we met had been a weaver but had to stop weaving because it was strenuous, took too long, and she could not make a living. She used to have the help of her daughter, but when her daughter moved to Bangkok to work in a factory she started putting together plastic flowers. She was not sure what her daughter was doing after the crisis, since she knew that the factory had closed down. All she knew was that her daughter was working for an uncle in the city.

It was interesting to observe the extent of the penetration of transnational capitalism. Far away from any urban center, a group of women sat in their backyards and made plastic flowers for a shop in the United States because weaving was no longer a viable way of making a living. The contrast between the inability of the weavers to capture either a domestic or an international market for their products and the ability of corporations to be able to penetrate the far reaches of Thailand to find workers able to assemble plastic flowers is striking.

Competing with Workers Worldwide

In the Philippines we again visited many garment workers. Here the market for their products was the United States. Many of the products had logos of U.S. universities and the labels from big retail shops. The women worked in small shops with very little light and no ventilation. As in Thailand, the children played in the shops and the workers got paid a piece-rate that was insufficient to live on. Interestingly, when trying to find out who the subcontractors were, something we did everywhere we went, the women kept talking about Bombay. It turned out that the subcontractors were from India. When I enquired further, I found out that some were Indian immigrants to the Philippines, but that others were working in the Philippines in order to circumvent the quotas imposed by the Multi-Fiber Agreement. According to this agreement each country has a quota imposed on it that limits its exports. Many of the women complained that they had lost work due to competition from Thailand and China. Some of them were self-employed but were not able to make a living. Subcontracted piece-rate work that used to be supplemental income had now become the only source of income. Some of the workers had originally migrated from other provinces to work in the factories and were unemployed and too poor to return home. The factory jobs offered benefits and social security. Many of the workers interviewed were now a part of an NGO and were part of an ongoing organizing strategy. According to these workers, globalization presented one the main problems they were confronting.

National Level

In Gujarat, India, we first visited a factory that made jeans for the domestic market. This was a large factory with about fifty workers. The workers all kept their belongings outside and were checked when they entered and left the factory premises. The cutters in the factory were all male and paid a wage, and the sewers were all women and were paid a piece-rate. There were no labels on the jeans, which we learned were sewn on in a separate room. Though this was also a subcontracted factory, the size of the factory and the number of employees made it fall under national labor regulations. This factory was much more like the global assembly line that has been studied extensively. The difference in the atmosphere of the factory and the small shop—in terms of human interaction—was stark. There was very little conversation (and there were no children playing with scissors). There was also external security and surveillance of the workers by management. It should be noted, however, that workers in small shops are also controlled—not by surveillance, but by their piece-rate-based earnings and the lack of a guarantee of payment. In talking to workers in several countries there existed some tension between the desire by many activists, particularly union organizers, to have work move back to a factory setting and the desire of workers to work near their homes in smaller settings with neighbors. The tension between the isolation and inability to organize has to be weighed against the problems women face in large factories. Recently many women were killed in a garment factory in Bangladesh because of hazardous work conditions and because the doors were locked to prohibit workers from leaving. This story keeps repeating itself through out the world. We need therefore to be more imaginative about forms of work that can capture some of the safety that working with neighbors or at home can bring with the need for workers to organize to protect their rights.

The Family

In Sri Lanka, about an hour outside of Colombo, we visited a manufacturer of wooden toys who sold them to a retailer in Europe. The owner of the factory explained that he preferred contract workers because when he had manufactured toys from a factory, the workers slowed down production during periods of high demand and asked for higher wages. Contract workers did not have the opportunity to organize and therefore he was better able to deal with market demand. He also explained that changes in the cost of materials were shared by him and the workers. The workers paid for the paints and other supplies while he provided the wood. This he felt would prevent waste and the workers would share in the rise in price of materials. The quality of the products were ensured since the workers only got paid for those toys that passed the quality inspection that was now conducted in the old factory. Many of the quality inspectors were male. Production was now organized around a number of small independently managed workshops, headed by women. These small shops were paid by piece, and the person who ran the center and worked alongside the other workers paid the other workers a piece-rate as well. As in Thailand, the workers know what piece-rate their neighbor received and what cut she got for providing the space and organizing the work. They were unaware, however, of the price that the owner got for the product.

In the company of the owner, we were then able to visit one of the small shops about an hour away. The women we spoke with were constrained in what they could say, given the owner's presence. They did state, however, that this work allowed them to be near home, to care for their children collectively, and maintain their household responsibilities. An unmarried woman was happy to be safe in her neighbor's house without having to travel to earn money before marriage. Though the work was not predictable and paid less than the minimum wage, the workers emphasized their need to have flexible work near their home. Another woman who was older used to work in a rubber plantation and was not able to physically continue working long hours and take care of her family. These workers were not a part of a national pension plan and had no guarantee of work from their employer.

In India we visited some home workers in Gujarat, who were sewing clothes for the domestic market. In some of the households the men had lost their jobs and now relied upon the income generated by the piece-rate work that the women performed. Many of the women said that they had their husbands working for them so they could earn more money. In this case, the gender relations in the household were changed due to women's control over subcontracted work.

> Here, capitalism's need for cheap labor allowed women a certain flexibility and con- trol over their wages. They were more vulnerable to the forces of the market both in terms of demand for the product as well as inflation, but they had easy access to their homes, and the company and help of the community of their neighbors. . . . Where social constraints on public mobility or when religious prohibition prevents women from leaving their community, such subcontracted work gives them a way to earn wages and change the power relations within the household. The forces of transna- tional capitalism simultaneously maintain and subvert the existing social structures: they uphold patriarchal constraints on women's mobility and change the gender dynamics in the family (Balakrishnan, 2000).

THE PROCESS

The visits described above were the beginning of a process that eventually led to this book. In each of the countries we visited we were taken to meet workers by NGOs who were organizing women. It was apparent that our ability to find workers, particu- larly home-based workers, could only be done by partnering with NGOs. We also real- ized that the NGO voice had to be integral to the design and implementation of the research. The process of conducting research is as important as the results of the research.

I would like this book to contribute not only to the growing literature in the field, but also to initiate a dialogue about the production of knowledge and the way in which academics and activists can engage as equal partners in producing work that is useful to both communities.

The process by which the research was shaped is significant to the cohesion of the book and the knowledge it attempts to produce. I would like to spend some time talking about this process because it was unique, and, for me personally, one of the more excit- ing aspects of this project. Unlike many edited books, where individuals write in iso- lation on certain topics and the editor shapes them to cohere with each other, this book is a product of a complex and challenging process.

After initially coming up with the broad research agenda of collecting data on the gendered dynamics of subcontracted work in the context of the global economy,

Margaret Huang and I traveled to Asia to identify research partners. As we were both living in the United States, we wanted a team of researchers located in the countries that we were focusing on. It was important to us that this research have a life in the country beyond the scope of this particular project. It was also important to have people share work in the region. All too often it is those of us who live and work in the North that have the privilege of knowing about work in many countries in the South. Though there has been increasing effort over the last decade in developing regional collaboration, it is still a rare occurrence.

Through the contacts of the Asia Foundation and personal contacts in several countries, we met with many groups of people. On reputation and instinct, we then put together teams in each country. In some cases it was the first time that a particular group of people had met, while in others, team members had enjoyed prior working relationships. In our attempt to keep this research grounded in advocacy we asked that NGOs be equal partners in the research team. We wanted to establish an equitable collaboration between researchers and activists.

During the autumn of 1998, research teams were established in each of the five participating countries: India, Pakistan, the Philippines, Sri Lanka, and Thailand. Each research team consisted of experts in macroeconomics and sociology or political science, as well as NGO advocacy, though in several of the teams academics were also NGO members. This combination provided strong macroeconomic and gender analysis while keeping the research grounded in the advocacy needs of the NGOs.

It was in this very initial phase that the research plan became more concrete. In almost every country, we took time to visit subcontracted workers and to conduct short interviews with several groups, so that the research could be informed by the anecdotal stories from workers. Meeting with researchers also helped determine the design of the research, in terms of what was actually feasible in a short period of time and with limited resources. We decided that in each country, 150 workers would be interviewed using a survey developed by each team.

A collaborative process was used to refine the conceptual framework of the research. We were interested in making links between macroeconomic dynamics and the increase of subcontracting in Asia. Through anecdotal evidence it became clear that women were the primary workers, particularly in small shops and home-based work. We limited our investigation to only those two categories of subcontracted workers. The surveys tried to ascertain the changes in household dynamics as a result of this work.

Making use of electronic communications, we clarified the initial conceptual framework with input from each of the teams, and finally came up with collective terms of reference (TOR) for the research. Each country team focused on those sectors that were important to their national context. The teams then established their own survey instruments and conducted a pilot study with a small sample of women workers. The surveys themselves were varied, based on the strengths of each team. The use of one survey for all five countries would have provided more comparable data, but the process of developing the survey to fit with national priorities, ongoing research, and activist interest seemed to us to be a more important long-term outcome.

At the end of this process, all the country teams met for the first time to collectively revise the TOR and include regional and international issues that had emerged. At this meeting, it was apparent that some of the issues—such as the gendered changes in time allocation and household budget expenditure—were not possible to capture in a large survey. We therefore decided to use focus groups and case studies to gather in-depth information that was not easy to ascertain from a survey. NGO members were trained to conduct the surveys, and in some instances the results of the findings were taken back to the workers and formed the basis of action workshops.

This meeting was crucial to the process, in that it established personal contacts and forged networks for advocacy that we hope will endure at the regional level and resulted in the articulation of problems involved in doing such research. The need for a multi-disciplinary approach was of crucial importance, but given that we generally work in a world that prioritizes a single discipline, translation across disciplines and differences between academic and activist priorities can sometimes prove challenging. Time was spent outside of the official meeting with individuals and individual teams, helping them to sort out any complicated working dynamics.

We met once again about seven months later—after the surveys were completed—to share research findings and, more importantly, to come up with policy implications of the five studies. We spent several days working in small groups broken up by country, discipline, and issues to emerge with a statement from each group that could be used for advocacy. There were quite a few differences in the policy strategies argued for at the national level, and we learned from each other. Several chapters in this book articulate advocacy strategies that NGOs have now employed at the national level.

CONCLUSION

The changing character of capitalist production has lead to the flexibilization of work, and changes in technology make decentralization of work commercially viable and efficient. Women, in order to incorporate their reproductive role, often accept unstable and vulnerable work. This flexibility has led to: greater insecurity; reduction in wages (though in many cases these women are new entrants to the labor force precisely because work has moved into the home); and lack of pension or any other forms of government benefits, over-time bonuses, holiday or maternity leave, sick pay, or insurance (Mitter 1994, 16).

Addressing the problems faced by these workers is not easy. Organizing subcontracted workers at the local level can be very difficult precisely for the reasons why companies increasingly prefer this kind of work. Any attempt at organizing is used by the employer to move to another location. In some instances, because the NGO that was helping gather data was well known, workers were afraid to be seen with its organizers for the fear of losing their contract. Their vulnerability as casual workers who are very difficult to find, makes organizing them very difficult. The familial relationship between the people who bring women work either to small shops or to their homes, once again decreases the ability and willingness to organize. In the places I visited it was also never clear whom to organize against. The shop managers, though making slightly higher piece-rates than the others, were not the focus of worker unrest. The workers had no idea where the work went and who was ultimately responsible for their working conditions.

Trade unions need to include informal sector workers and, in particular, subcontracted workers, to ensure that all are not pitted against organized formal sector workers. Unions should try to adopt a one-union/one-industry concept of organizing that includes all workers. It is important to note, however, that many subcontracted workers work in multiple industries in order to support their families year-round. Many NGOs had a hard time working with some of the traditional trade unions, since subcontracted workers were perceived as scab workers. Unions also need to, in many instances, see beyond a large factory model of organizing. More understanding of the industry-specific gender variations in the informal and formal sector is necessary, as well as the gender-specific dimensions of incorporating paid and unpaid work.

For many policy makers, the best means available to improve the economic situation of subcontracted workers, and women in general, seemed to lie in providing access to microcredit. Policy makers hoped that providing subcontracted workers with the necessary capital would enable them to become independent small-scale entrepreneurs. The problems with this response, however, are many. The larger economic changes that put women in these vulnerable positions in the first place remain salient.

Power relations in the household as well as in society have to be addressed. At the same time, focusing only on the social and cultural problems faced by women in many countries can divert attention away from broader macroeconomic forces and firm-level decisions that exacerbate these tensions. While advocacy at the international level might not take into account the particular needs of a community of workers, local level advocacy might be ineffective against the power of national and global macroeconomic policies. Given increased global economic integration, policy advocates need to become more effective at making links from the local to the international levels.

It is also important to recognize the relationship between specific macroeconomic policy and the effect that it has on working conditions, particularly for women. Feminist economists have brought attention to the policy biases inherent in the fact that women's unpaid reproductive work was invisible because it is not a part of the cash economy (Bakker 1999). Similarly the hidden nature of subcontracted work can lead to policies that are detrimental to women workers. Their contribution to the larger economy, though part of the commodity chain, is not seen or measured.

International efforts that bring attention to the plight of workers often end up harming the very workers in whose interest they seek to advance. For example, consumer campaigns in the North that boycott products made in sweatshop conditions often have the effect of denying poor women access to even these meager wages. International campaigns need to be in closer touch with the organizers on the ground to respond to worker demands.

It is also crucial to examine the growing movement by corporations to adopt socially responsible practices. Under these initiatives, corporations require that the manufacturers whom they contract work to sign agreements that bind them, in principle, to pay legal wages and maintain proper working environments. Corporations frequently complain that they have done as much as they can do, and that it is impossible for them to monitor the practices of the manufacturers who themselves further subcontract out the work. This position conveniently overlooks the narrow profit margins these corporations force the manufacturer to work with, which often sets in motion a calculated scramble to reduce labor costs. Though I commend any corporation for taking an interest in the working conditions of workers, they are unwilling to address the central problem, which is their profit-making strategy. The sharing of risk among all the participants in the commodity chain will have a negative effect on the lives of the workers.

A larger intergovernmental body to ensure the rights of workers against the business interests of capital must be established. Though the International Labor Organization (ILO) exists—and due to pressure from workers there has now been recognition of the specific need to address home-workers—the ILO has little power to implement labor regulations (Prugel 1999). With the increasing power of the World Trade Organization (WTO) there is a need to establish a counter-balancing organization that has the ability and will to limit the power of corporations. The ILO itself needs to be strengthened and mandated to play a more powerful role. There also needs to be a UN body as there was in the past whose mandate is to watch over the abuse of power by Transnational corporations, in terms of issues broader than just labor.

In the context of these larger organizing concerns, this book brings together a collection of essays that examine the relationship between subcontracted work and the changes in the global economy.

Chapter 2 places subcontracting in a global context and provides a theoretical framework to help understand the reasons behind the increasing use of subcontracted work both nationally and internationally. The concept of push and pull are used to describe the reasons why certain industries and countries move toward subcontracted work. The gendered aspect of the labor market is examined to explain the overwhelming use of women in this sector, as well as some of the reasons why many women interviewed preferred this work. Balakrishnan and Sayeed focus on Pakistan, but also use macroeconomic information from other countries to make some generalizations about the relationship between macroeconomic policies and subcontracted work.

Chapter 3 looks at the relationship between women's access to paid work and the expectation of empowerment. Khattak questions whether patriarchal structures are broken down by the increase in women's paid employment or whether particular forms of employment inscribe them further. Using data collected in Pakistan, this chapter shows how subcontracted work maintains women's marginal economic status, as well as preserving social constraints on women's mobility. This chapter also critically reviews organizing strategies aimed at advancing women workers' interests and argues for a concerted effort on the part of civil society institutions such as community-based organizations, non-governmental organizations, the media, the government, and international development institutions to help subcontracted women workers.

Chapter 4 is premised on the belief that there is an interdependence among macroeconomic policies, the ground realities of economic and social relations of production, and the economic behavior of households. To illustrate this, Jayaweera examines five areas of subcontracted work in Sri Lanka: electronics, garments/embroidery, coir, agro-based production and urban construction. Her research provides a detailed look at these industries in order to situate the position of subcontracted workers within the domestic economy. The chapter pays special attention to the effects of subcontracted work on gender roles and gender relations.

Chapter 5 looks at the policy and program implications of the financial crisis on subcontracted women workers in the Philippines. Ofreneo, Lim, and Guha focus on the garment industry to examine the impact of the crisis on the changing structure of employment. Based on the example of the National Network of Home Workers (PATAMABA), they maintain that community-based organizing is the key to empowering women workers. The authors provide information culled from interviews and focus groups to show the real-life consequences of the macroeconomic downturns.

Chapter 6 analyzes how the changes in the garment industry affect the situation of women in subcontracting arrangements. Unni and Bali provide a multi-tiered investigation of the impact of the changes in the garment industry in Ahmedabad, India, on women workers. They connect their analysis to a direct organizing strategy now employed by the Self Employed Women's Association (SEWA) to achieve self-reliance through joint strategies of struggle and development.

Women are the most marginalized workers in the informal sector. It is our hope that the issues raised in this book constitute a starting point for uncovering additional information about the lives of these hidden workers. Given the growth of subcontracted work around the world, it is of critical importance to continue research that understands how workers, particularly women, strategize around prevalent macroeconomic forces. We hope that the examples of advocacy strategies presented here will inform further struggles in other contexts.

NOTES

1. Margaret Huang was the Program director for the Asia Foundation during the time the original research that this book comments on was done. Ms. Huang and I traveled together and worked closely together for several years. I use "we" in this chapter to include the enormous contribution that Margaret made to the design of the research.

2. Subcontracted work is defined by the ILO as an industrial or commercial practice whereby the party placing the contract requests another enterprise or establishment (the subcontractor) to manufacture or process parts of the whole of a product or products that it sells as its own.

3. Though Thailand was a part of the original research, there is no chapter from Thailand in this book.

REFERENCES

Bakker, Isabella. 1999. Neoliberal Governance and the New Gender Order. In *Working Papers* Vol.1 No.1.

Balakrishnan, Radhika. 2000. Capitalism and Sexuality: Free to Choose? In *Good Sex: Feminist Perspectives on World Religion*, edited by Jung, Hunt and Balakrishnan. New Brunswick: Rutgers University Press.

Beneria, Lourdes and Martha Roldan. 1985. *The Cross Roads of Class and Gender: Industrial Homework, Subcontracting, and Household Dynamics in Mexico City*. Chicago: University of Chicago Press.

Feldman, F. and Eveline Ferretti. 1998. Informal Work: A Critique of Prevailing Views. In *Informal Work and Social Change: A Bibliographic Survey*, edited by Feldman and Ferretti. Ithaca: Cornell University Press.

Hsiung, Ping-Chun. 1996. *Living Rooms as Factories: Class, Gender, and the Satellite Factory system in Taiwan*. Philadelphia: Temple University Press.

Mitter, Swasti. 1994. On Organizing in Casualised Work: A Global Overview. In *Dignity and Daily Bread*, edited by Rowbotham and Mitter. London: Routledge.

Ong Aihwa. 1997. The Gender Labor Politics of Post Modernity. In *The Politics of Culture in the Shadow of Capital*, edited by Lowe and Lloyd. Durham: Duke University Press.

Prugl, Elisabeth. 1999. *The Global Construction of Gender: Home-based work in the Political Economy of the 20th Century*. New York: Columbia University Press.

2

Subcontracting: The Push-Pull Factor

Radhika Balakrishnan and Asad Sayeed

There have been significant changes in the form of industrial production over the last few decades. Flexibilization of production has disintegrated the production process while integrating the world economy through trade. As manufacturing or service activities performed abroad are now combined with activities performed at home, companies are finding it profitable to outsource increasing amounts of the production process. The rise in outsourcing, whether domestically or internationally oriented, represents a breakdown in the vertically integrated mode of production—the so-called "Fordist" production process[1] (Feenstra 1998, 2). There is a need therefore to "examine cycles and trends in the relationship between positions in the global distribution of labor and the spatial distribution and disintegration of the production process" (Korzeniewicz and Martin 1994, 68). In addition, the global distribution of labor is gendered, and it is important to understand the change in the sexual division of labor brought about by the change in the production process.

The conceptual analysis that follows stems from our efforts to contextualize and understand the phenomenon of subcontracted female workers in five Asian economies: Pakistan, India, Sri Lanka, Thailand and the Philippines. We seek to gain insights into the relationship between gender and national and international macroeconomic policies.

This chapter focuses on Pakistan as a clear example of how the push factor dominates, and we explore the relationship between macroeconomic policy and the gender dimensions of changing labor conditions. We then survey four other countries to look at some common macroeconomic changes that have taken place in each of these countries. We also wanted to provide a brief overview to help place the other chapters in context.

One of the most notable changes in industrial production over the last forty years is the substantial decrease in some of the traditional costs of production. Specifically, transportation and communication costs have fallen dramatically. Between 1960 and

1990, operating costs per mile for the world's airlines fell by 60%. Between 1970 and 1999, the cost of an international telephone call fell by 90%, and today Internet technology is dramatically decreasing the cost of communicating internationally. In addition, a traditional cost of trading has been reduced with the easing of trade barriers; in 1947, the average tariff on manufactured imports was 47%, but with the full implementation of the Uruguay round it should fall to 3% (United Nations Development Programme/UNDP Human Development Report 1997).

There has also been a change in the process of production, particularly in those goods where large retailers have set up decentralized production networks in a wide range of exporting countries. Such flexibilization provides the manufacturers with a competitive edge, as they benefit from the physical presence of numerous suppliers in different locations, particularly small firms, factories, small shops and home-based work. We looked at subcontracted labor as a process whereby the manufacturer externalizes many of the costs associated with the labor process (Appelbaum and Gereffi 1994, 45).

It is important to conceptually clarify some of the determinants leading to the disintegration of the production process and the consequent rise in subcontracting. Such a conceptual analysis will help to distinguish various forms of subcontracting arrangements and to better understand the different impacts on labor.

The "push-pull" framework is a useful explanatory device in the context of the debate about subcontracting. Those who celebrate subcontracting (Piore and Sabel 1984; Williamson 1985; and others) argue that decentralizing productions creates more jobs and hence, opportunities for women. They argue that over time their wages and working conditions will improve. On the other hand, critics of subcontracting argue that the process is exploitative, particularly for women (Beneria and Roldan 1987; Mitter 1994; Ong 1997). We try to conceptually clarify this debate by introducing the "push-pull" mechanisms at work. We argue that macro changes over the last decade or two in developing countries has shown that, though the pull factors exist, the push factor has dominated.

In essence, subcontracting is a change in the Fordist pattern of the division of labor associated with mass production. The disintegration of the production process toward subcontracting can be conceptualized as occurring either due to *push* or *pull* factors. Here we use the terms push and pull to refer to the reasons why a particular industry might decide to outsource its production. Understanding the incentive to subcontract gives us some grasp of the impact on labor of this phenomenon, including the manner in which it impacts on employment, wages, and working conditions.

The defining feature of a *pull* towards subcontracting is its productivity-enhancing character.[2] The simplest pull mechanism towards subcontracting is the principle of expanded reproduction, which states that the division of labor is determined by the extent of the market. As demand for a particular industry increases, the minimum efficient scale of those products used as inputs increases and leads to that product being manufactured independently (Stigler 1968). This form of subcontracting is generally associated with capital-intensive, continuous-flow methods of production and is amenable to production technologies where economies of scale are central.

The above form of subcontracting, however, is different from subcontracting in sectors where technology is generally based on batch production—where the production process is broken down into distinct and fully contained tasks. Labor- and/or skill-intensive sectors dominate this profile. In these sectors, innovations in the division of labor occur either due to technological change or changes in organizational strategies to minimize transaction and/or labor costs. Subcontracting offers a reduction in monitoring costs and thereby enhances labor productivity. Monitoring costs are reduced either by piece-rating or by shifting work to smaller units where supervision of the labor input is relatively easy. Examples of this form of subcontracting are generally associated with manufacture of consumer goods, such as garments, footwear (at the higher value-added end[3]), and carpets, but consulting services and software design are also demonstrative of this form of disintegration of the production process. Whether increasing labor productivity translates into higher returns to labor depends on the prevailing degree of labor market segmentation among the skilled and unskilled, and among men and women, as well as the existence of and compliance with labor laws. In the countries surveyed, a priori, it is expected that labor market segmentation will be high and legal cover for workers will either be weak or bypassed routinely.

Even in a segmented market with virtually no legal coverage for workers, however, employment conditions can improve through subcontracting in skill-intensive sectors.[4] This depends on two factors: the relative ease or difficulty of imparting skills, and the level of demand for the final product. If imparting skills is relatively cheap and/or not time consuming,[5] then wages will remain depressed as the supply of adequately skilled labor increases. If skill development is costly and time consuming, then improvements in wages and working conditions can be expected. This polarization of skill has a gender dimension; women are generally relegated to the low-skilled or semi-skilled positions (Standing 1989). Similarly if demand for the final product is growing (particularly if demand growth is export led), then the labor supply may constrict and wages may increase. But this may be at the cost of employment generation, especially of women. In short, improvements in working conditions depend on the particular configuration in the interplay between skill development and growth in demand. The former factor is very often differentiated by sex, as women are usually not given skill development training and often remain in sectors that are low skilled and easily replaceable (Standing 1989). It is important, therefore, to see which sectors of subcontracted work rely upon women workers and which do not. Evidence has shown that in the export processing zones, particularly in Asia, women were drawn into the labor force primarily in low-skilled work for short periods of time (Beneria 1999). These findings were echoed in our own research in industries that subcontracted women workers.

Subcontracting in technology-intensive sectors is based on bringing together general purpose and divisible machinery with skilled and trained workers.[6] Thus, both capital and labor productivity increases. Divisibility of capital makes it cost-effective for the large firm to outsource such activities and reap the gains from economies of specialization (Williamson 1985). Software development, computer designing,[7] manufacture of automobile parts, and electronics are examples of such activity. Again, extremely skilled labor is a prerequisite for this phenomenon to emerge. As such, it remains confined to a small portion of the workforce—usually male—in developing countries.

The pull towards subcontracting seems to be determined by a mix of technological and skill-related factors. At the upper end of the spectrum, wages and working conditions for highly skilled workers improve. At the lower end of the spectrum, the particular mix of skill development and demand determines whether there is improvement in wages and working conditions.

In contrast to the pull towards subcontracting, firms can be *pushed* into outsourcing because of increasing economic costs, excessive competition, or in order to circumvent labor legislation. Production of consumer non-durables at the lower end of the market segment and much of home-based work are examples of the *push* into subcontracting. The outsourced work process is usually the least skill-intensive, involving minimal capital outlays, and the labor process is generally repetitive and monotonous. Rather than improving productivity and product quality, reducing costs to survive in the market is the dominant criterion. Push is generally due to macroeconomic conditions and can be seen as a "coping" strategy on the part of firms to either stay in business or to maintain their profit levels. For example, firms are pushed into subcontracting as a response to increasing economic costs of production, including a rise in the cost of land or utilities, exchange rate pressures, and capital costs. Since the overall increase in production costs is beyond the control of individual entrepreneurs, they resort to reducing labor and overhead costs by outsourcing those aspects of the production process wherever it is technologically and administratively feasible to do so.[8] Such outsourcing will not necessarily lead to any productivity enhancement, and the expected impact on wages and working conditions could be negative.

High levels of competition in the product market also push firms into disintegrating the production process. At the lower end of the market spectrum,[9] where lower cost rather than quality is the determining criterion for capturing market share, cost reduction takes place through subcontracting work, typically to home-based workers. It is important to note that this kind of competition is largely a result of liberalization, where entry barriers for firms or finished products in the market are either absent or have been eliminated by tariff reductions and/or deregulation of investment decisions. Because liberalization has been adopted in many developing countries, push subcontracting is a frequent phenomenon in many industries.

Only a small segment of the third world consumer market corresponds to the quality-conscious western consumer, where niche markets for customized products are increasingly ruling the roost. In such markets, healthy "competition" exists, where quality and design, rather than price, is the determining factor. Much of the consumerism in the developing world is based on either cheap (read affordable) imitations or "modern" necessities. As tariff barriers come down, intra-third world competition for imitation Gucci handbags or Levi jeans or simply casual garments or toothbrushes, soaps, and slippers intensifies. And since price is the only criterion through which market share is to be captured among these labor-intensive industries, a veritable competition ensues between poor countries over whose labor is cheapest. If the Pakistani slipper maker is to survive on the back streets of Karachi selling her product, she has to pay less to her worker than her Chinese or Vietnamese counterpart. The bottom line is thus clearly defined. Niches in this case shift from products to workers. Employers/producers then prowl for women and children of the poorest households, who are usually migrants either from rural areas or from war-ravaged or calamity-hit neighboring countries. Once such segmentation in the labor market is intensified, then the wage rate in the labor market as a whole also drops. If the producers are successful in reducing the overall wage level, then in popular parlance they have attained competitiveness.

The push towards subcontracting is, therefore, primarily motivated by reducing labor costs and is not necessarily productivity enhancing. Reduction in labor costs, in turn, is only achievable either by circumventing labor laws (informalizing employment), or by changing the contractual arrangement in a way that is beyond the ambit of legislation.[10] In most of the industries examined, women subcontracted workers were employed for low-skilled work, and therefore experienced many negative effects of this increasing change in the production process. These industries employ a higher percentage of women workers and are spatially located in small shops or home-based venues; the mix of skill level and the decreasing demand for these products results in low wages for the workers and no skill enhancement.

MACROECONOMIC CHANGES

In Pakistan, the Philippines, Thailand, Sri Lanka, and India, the 1990s brought about a period of increased liberalization and export-orientation growth. The move toward subcontracting in a majority of the countries has been accompanied by a disintegration of the production process in several sectors. There have been various macroeconomic policy changes encouraging a move away from large-scale industrial production and a promotion of medium-scale and small-scale production. This policy has often led to outsourcing by large factories as well as efforts by subcontractors to start small-scale industries to attract foreign companies to outsource production.

Government regulation of labor or the lack of it, as well as increased international and domestic competition, has led many industries to lower the costs of production by using decentralized production and labor that is not part of the regulated formal sector. Though each country has had a unique trajectory in terms of macroeconomic changes, the similarity in liberalization policies is striking. In the particular industries examined there is a clear link between macroeconomic policy and increases in sub-contracting relationships driven primarily by push factors. Furthermore, the impact on labor and particularly women workers has resulted in a rise in low-skilled, low-waged employment.

An extensive review of the macroeconomic changes in all the countries is beyond the scope of this chapter, instead we provide a brief overview of macroeconomic changes in these five countries to bring attention to some of the cross-cutting macro indicators that have lead to an increase in subcontracted work and the feminization of this work. Financial market liberalization has resulted in increasing interest rates that provides incentive to firms to subcontract/outsource their production. Tariff reduction increases domestic competition that again prompts firms to reduce labor costs (both wage and non-wage) by subcontracting. Incentives to export in labor intensive industries has generally resulted in labor polarization and has increased vulnerability of workers, particularly women workers. Deregulations of the labor market and the implicit allowance to bypass existing legislation have increased low-wage employment, consisting of jobs paying individual rather than family wages, making women particularly vulnerable. (Standing 1989). Privatization/downsizing in government (one of the largest employers in these countries) has increased distress sale of labor, particularly of women.[11]

Pakistan

A significant and enduring political-economic development in Pakistan during the early 1990s was the liberalization of the economy. For much of that decade, economic policies were dictated by the specific conditionalities of the structural adjustment programs (SAPs) introduced under the aegis of the International Monetary Fund (IMF). This macroeconomic environment has been a significant factor in how the incentive structure for subcontracting work has been shaped.

The central element of liberalization has been the deregulation of prices in the economy so that allocation of resources is determined by the market and is in accordance with relative factor scarcities. Three key prices that were deregulated were domestic prices, interest rates, and the exchange rate. Domestic price liberalization meant that administered prices, which entail either an absolute subsidy (such as fertilizer, wheat, and edible oils) or cross-subsidies (such as those on agricultural produce, electricity, gas, etc.), were to be gradually phased out. Reductions in the subsidies on utilities, especially electricity and gas, resulted in a stiff increase in the price of these essential public goods. Between 1991 and 1997, electricity and gas tariffs increased at a rate of 20.9% and 16.5% per annum respectively, while the average price on petroleum products increased at a rate of 20% per annum.

As a result of financial liberalization, interest rates on long-term projects increased from an average of 12% per annum in 1990 to an average of 20–23% per annum in 1997 (Zaman Associates 1997, 46). Similarly, the interest rates on working capital have also increased to 20–25% per annum in this period.[12] This steep increase in the interest rate was a result of two policy measures carried out under the aegis of liberalization. One, as mentioned above, was the policy to deregulate the interest rate and remove all forms of interest subsidy on capital. Having deregulated the interest, a tight monetary policy was initiated. Both of these factors then resulted in a steep increase in the interest rate.

Interest rates on working capital also increased to 20–25% per annum in this period. Although the exchange rate was liberalized from a fixed peg to a "managed float" in 1982, exchange rate devaluation was initiated in earnest only after the financial sector reforms in 1991. Whereas the average rate of devaluation of the rupee in the 1980s was a mere 8% per annum, between 1991 and 1999 this increased to a massive 21% per annum on average.

Partly as a result of liberalization measures initiated earlier and partly due to past neglect, the fiscal deficit of the state became unsustainable. This was a "double whammy" for the formal manufacturing sector. In the zeal to reduce expenditure and increase revenues, the state resorted to slashing public expenditure in infrastructure on the expenditure side.[13] Public infrastructure—such as roads, electricity provision, communication facilities, etc.—not only crowds in private investment, but also creates positive externalities for private investment. As a result, the cost curve for formal manufacturing units indirectly became steeper.

On the expenditure side, several indirect taxes were introduced, again under pressure from the IMF. The most prominent of these was the General Sales Tax (GST). Although by definition the tax is value-added—and therefore the producer passes on the cost to the next phase in the production cycle and eventually to the consumer— it immensely increased transaction costs for the producer.

All of these factors have led to an increase in the economic costs for manufacturers. It is therefore possible to conjecture that the push mechanism towards subcontracting is expected to increase in the Pakistan economy. This theory is further corroborated by deceleration in the economy, and more significantly, in the manufacturing sector. In the absence of other direct welfare measures undertaken by the state, economic growth has helped generate employment and is primarily responsible for improvements in per-capita incomes and living standards. However, in recent years gross domestic product (GDP) has decelerated from an average of 7% per annum in the 1980s to 4% in the 1990–2000 period.

Growth in large-scale manufacturing has decelerated considerably from an average 8.7% per annum between 1980–91 to a mere 3.9% per annum between 1990–99.[14] Since the onset of liberalization, growth in exports has decelerated as well, compared to a decade earlier. While growth in primary commodity exports has slightly increased, no improvements can be discerned in manufactured exports. The share of non-traditional exports actually declined in the 1988–98 period to 27% of total exports, compared to the 1977–88 period when it was 30% (SPDC 1999, 7). There is thus no evidence that resources have been re-allocated toward the external sector as a result of liberalization. To the extent that subcontracting arrangements that emerge in the wake of export-led growth are productivity enhancing, this has not occurred in the case of Pakistan.

Apart from organizational and technological considerations, there is little pressure on the employer, given the deregulated and segmented state of the labor market. All labor laws are only applicable on industries employing more than 10 workers and those that are registered.[15] Even if it is a specialized task, the non-wage labor cost as well as the overhead is reduced for the employer, adding little to the productivity of the labor process.

As discussed earlier, a push into subcontracting at the lower end of the market spectrum is due to excessive competition brought about by reduced tariff barriers for finished products. While the process of removal of tariff and non-tariff barriers in the economy was initiated in the early 1980s, the 1990s saw the swiftest reduction in tariff ceilings. From a maximum tariff rate of 225% in 1986–87, the maximum rate was brought down to 125% by 1988–89, to 65% in 1996, 45% in 1997, and subsequently to 35% in March 1999. This has damaged the intermediate goods industry—particularly light engineering—and a number of consumer goods, such as footwear, utensils, crockery and cutlery, cosmetics and toiletries, etc.[16]

Aggregate labor force data in Pakistan are of poor quality, inconsistent, and are published with a considerable time lag. As such, reliable information cannot be extracted. However, given that it is the only source of information, this study referred to the data in an attempt to gauge the impact of macroeconomic changes on subcontracting. The share of manufacturing employment declined marginally in the 1990s. Since subcontracting is expected to appear in the small-scale sector, the relevant data would likely be found in this category. Aggregate data, however, do not tell us the division of employment between large- and small-scale sectors. The last year for which disaggregated information on employment is available (1990–91) shows that the division of employment between large and small-scale sectors at that time was 25% and 75% respectively.[17] Over the last nine years, however, the small-scale share was expected to increase, simply because growth in the large-scale sector (for which information is available) has decelerated considerably. Even if incremental employment generation in the 1990s occurred in the small-scale sector, it still does not necessarily imply that this employment has been generated in subcontracting industries. Thus, aggregate data do not provide any conclusive evidence to the prevalence of subcontracting within manufacturing.

If aggregate, labor-force data are problematic; the data on women workers are even weaker. As Kazi notes, "Most standard labor force data, including the population census and the labor force surveys, are known to greatly underestimate the extent of female labor force participation.... [Also problematic are] Inappropriate definitions of what is considered economic activity and questions which lay stress on recording a single main activity, as well as unsuitable methods of data collection where usually both enumerators and respondents are males. In the Pakistani context, where women perform multiple tasks and where there are social inhibitions to admitting to women's work, these procedures lead to under-remuneration of the female labor force, (Kazi 1999, 385-386)."

The lack of data is most apparent where participation of urban women in the labor force was shown to have taken a sudden jump, and then tapered off after 1991.[18] Similarly, the share of women among the employed labor force in urban areas continues to be extremely low. This is perhaps due to the non-reporting of female work, particularly home-based work. Since there is evidence from several surveys that the bulk of urban employment among women is generated in the informal sector and particularly among home-based workers,[19] the unambiguous conclusion is that female labor force participation is underestimated. Given this basic lack of data, it is virtually impossible to discern aggregate patterns of subcontracted work among the female labor force.

There are several other reasons, however, which point toward increasing participation of women in the labor force in the 1990s. First, increasing literacy among women is expected to have increased their participation in the labor force. Between the 1981 and 1999 censuses, the proportion of literate women older than 10 years in the urban areas increased from 37.3% to 55.6% (Economic Survey 1999, 125). While literacy does not necessarily imply participation in the labor force, it is undeniable that increasing literacy will result in increasing labor force participation, though the elasticity between literacy and labor force participation may be low in Pakistan for cultural reasons.

As part of the liberalization package, the government vigorously pursued privatization soon after it launched its liberalization drive in 1991. In the first phase, industrial units within the fold of the public sector were earmarked for privatization. Of the 109 industrial units in the public sector, 82 were privatized by 1996. According to the Government of Pakistan (1999), employment in public industrial enterprises declined from 73,565 workers in 1991–92 to 43,425 workers by December 1997. Linked to privatization, the state is also concentrating on downsizing government departments as well as public sector entities. Downsizing in public sector corporations has been substantial. Between 1991 and 1998, employment in the public sector has been halved— from 514,620 employees to 258,780 (Government of Pakistan 1999). Since the bulk of this retrenchment consists of men, more women are expected to have entered the labor force to protect household incomes.

The period of economic liberalization has also coincided with increasing poverty trends in Pakistan.[20] On all different indices of poverty,[21] the incidence of poverty in Pakistan consistently declined through the 1970s and 1980s. In the 1990s, however, this trend reversed. Again, there is almost complete unanimity among numerous empirical studies that demonstrate this trend.[22] An increase in poverty inevitably leads to an increase in labor supply, especially of women who have never worked before. As skills among the poorest of women are assumed to be low, they are expected to occupy the lowest rungs of paid employment. When coupled with the evidence of firms being pushed into subcontracting, women sell their labor in distress and take up these jobs.

The Philippines

The Philippines began the 1990s with an enormous foreign debt, high interest rates, and a tight monetary policy imposed by the International Monetary Fund (IMF). President Ramos's government liberalized the foreign exchange and capital accounts and deepened the privatization and liberalization efforts started by the Aquino government. There was also a further deregulation of key industries exhibiting an increase in productivity and growth. The Philippines also joined the World Trade Organization (WTO), the ASEAN Free Trade Area (AFTA), and the Asia-Pacific Economic Cooperation (APEC), while unilaterally reducing tariffs ahead of most of its neighbors. The last decade also witnessed intense export competition from low-cost production countries such as China, India, Bangladesh, Sri Lanka, Indonesia, Eastern European countries, Mexico, and the Caribbean Basin countries.

It is in this context of intense foreign competition in both the external (export) market and the internal (domestic) market that the push toward subcontracting has been given a new dimension. Due to uncompetitive labor costs (a result of previous high inflation rates that led to a high cost of living), labor-management conflicts (especially in garments, textile, chemical, and pharmaceutical plants), and flexible firm size (to improve on efficiency), subcontracting and related practices have become coping mechanisms for firms. According to the Survey on Specific Group of Workers (SSGW) released by the Bureau of Labor and Employment Statistics (BLES) of the Department of Labor and Employment (DOLE), between 1994 and 1997 (at the height of trade competition) the number of registered subcontracting firms increased by 51.5%, from 361 to 547 (Diaz 1999). The subcontracting firms, however, are often large establishments employing many workers on a firm-basis rather than on a home-basis. Export-oriented firms, as well as firms with foreign partners, tend to subcontract part of their production more often than other types of firms (Diaz 1999).

Though there has been an increase in subcontracting, there has also been a slowdown in garment industry production affecting women workers. Garments, footwear, wood manufactures, baby carriages, toys, games and sporting goods, basketwork, wickerwork and other articles of plaiting materials, and miscellaneous manufactured articles (including *papier mâché*) showed low-growth rates. These are precisely the sectors where many women home-based and subcontracted workers are employed, and are industries where the push factor is more prominent. Garment exports in particular have stagnated such that their share of exports fell from 21.7% of the total in 1990 to a mere 8% in 1998. Garments were replaced by machinery and transport equipment as the second top export earner (after semiconductors and electronic parts) starting in 1997.

Garments comprised 17.5% of total manufacturing employment in 1988. In 1998, this figure declined to around 15%. Textiles, on the other hand, comprised 7.9% of manufacturing employment in 1988, and this number declined to 5.6% in 1998. The garment sector is the second largest employer in manufacturing after food production, while the textiles industry is the fourth largest employer in manufacturing after electrical machinery and apparatus. It is important to note, however, that the statistics on the number of employees are grossly underestimated since they are based on the results of a survey by the National Statistics Office (NSO) of formal establishments employing 10 workers and above. Though official statistics capture certain sectors of the labor market, they fail to account for the informal sector activity, small-shop, and home-based employment. The NSO survey did not capture employment in firms with less than 10 workers, i.e., firms and workers in the informal sector including home-based workers. In contrast, the Garments and Textile Export Board (GTEB) estimates that there are close to one million workers in the garment industry if subcontracted and home workers are counted. This could indicate that though official measures of employment indicate a decrease, firms have been pushed to subcontracting to small shops and home-based work as a cost-cutting measure brought about by excessive competition in the international market.

Thailand

After many years of following an import substitution industrialization policy, in the early 1970s, Thailand moved toward an export-led growth model. By the late 1980s, the region's growth was heavily dependent on Japanese direct investment. By the beginning of the 1990s, Thailand experienced an impressive overall economic growth rate exceeding 10% in some years. The industrial sector was targeted for enhanced growth, and by the mid-1990s, industrial exports accounted for approximately 70% of Thailand's GDP. As Japanese investment started to taper off, alternate sources of capital had to be tapped, particularly international banks looking for higher yields on their loans and mutual funds, and other speculative institutions searching for more profitable investments than were elsewhere available.

Thailand's strategy to attract foreign investment led to the liberalization of the financial sector, maintenance of high domestic interest rates to bring in portfolio investment and bank capital, and pegging of the currency to the dollar to reassure foreign investors against currency risk. Net portfolio investment totaled some $24 billion in the early 1990s, while another $50 billion entered as loans to Thai banks and enterprises. This capital, however, was not focused on the domestic manufacturing sector or agriculture but rather the stock market, consumer financing, and, in particular, real estate (FOCUS-on-Trade 1998).

In the early 1990s, the government of Thailand, through the Bank of Thailand (BOT), deregulated the financial sector. First, under the terms of an agreement with the IMF, the BOT loosened foreign exchange control to allow foreign and domestic capital to move more freely. In 1993, the Bangkok International Banking Facilities (BIBF) was established to facilitate foreign funds. These measures and the ensuing economic boom encouraged large numbers of foreign investors to invest in Thailand. The investment resulted in high liquidity and lower interest rates, which were important factors stimulating domestic aggregate demand. However, the capital influx was mostly short-term. A large part of foreign savings was invested in the stock market and part of it was loaned to local businesses. Easy credit was given to several types of businesses. Large credit, however, was distributed to the real estate sector, which speculated heavily.

Along with financial deregulation, the government also pursued a new industrial policy in the early 1990s. In 1992, decentralized industry and rural industry were promoted. These steps were intended to reduce economic inequality between the rural and urban populations and to discourage labor migration from rural areas. The government gave several incentives to industries that settled or relocated in rural zones, including tax cuts in business income, duty cuts for imported raw materials, and easy credit to rural enterprises. Moreover, numerous basic facilities were created for the industrial zones mentioned above. Target industries were those that exported, created a large number of community jobs, and intensively utilized local raw materials (the garment industry is one example). Besides these tools, the government also supported expansion of subcontracted work to rural areas.

In the same year, 1992, the Department of Export Promotion encouraged the Thai garment industry to improve the quality of its products because lower quality garment products faced strong competition from new emerging suppliers such as China and Indonesia. The encouragement, however, was arranged through capital-intensive methodology, i.e., the greater efficiency generated by the new machinery. The Department of Business Economics reported that this development resulted in 7–10% of workers being laid off.

The rapid expansion of export production in Thailand and the high competition in the world market at the end of the 1980s and in the early 1990s pushed industrial entrepreneurs to lower their production costs. Technological innovation and the use of machines to replace labor-intensive work were encouraged in the large and medium industries. Industrial production using labor-intensive techniques was allocated to small-scale enterprises, often contracted out to those with lower costs of production, which encouraged subcontracting.

As a result of the boom in external demand, easy loans, and other supported policies, the textile and garment industries expanded and hence needed more workers. However, these industries faced stronger competition. Many new countries came on the scene with cheaper labor costs (about 25% of Thai cost) and other resources, while Thailand was in the opposite situation. The minimum wage rate (nominal) increased every year while low labor productivity remained. Moreover, AFTA caused Thailand to impose duty reductions. It appears that foreign garments (especially from China) captured a large domestic market share.

Along with these factors, a strong baht, due to the export boom and influx of foreign capital, also depressed Thailand's competitiveness. To cope with strong competition, businesses imposed cost-cutting strategies such as downsizing (laying off workers), relocating to border regions (employing cheap labor from neighboring countries like Myanmar), and increasing labor flexibility through subcontracting. Consequently, the number of formal sector workers declined. A large proportion of work was subcontracted to informal labor, which accepted lower wages. These policies and measurements contributed to an increase in subcontracting work in the garment industry.

In 1997, the financial crisis in Thailand caused many medium and large-scale industries to go out of business. In the initial period of the economic crisis, over 75% of the workers laid off were from labor-intensive industries such as textiles, shoes, toys, frozen foods, and jewelry (Kokit 1997). Although subcontracting had existed in Thailand during the earlier boom period, the crisis spurred many large employers to close their factories and contract out the work to small subcontracted firms as a cost-cutting measure.

The garment industry, in Thailand, was targeted by the Thai government as a sector for export promotion. Both domestic and foreign capital investors were given incentives to invest in this sector. Though the number of firms in this industry grew in the early 1990s, the number of formal sector jobs did not increase by very much. The employment rate in the garment sector increased by only 2.3% from 1992 to 1995. There was a sharp decline of over 20% in the value of garment exports in 1996, primarily due to competition from other low-wage countries in this sector. Because of the increased competition, many factories closed shop and moved some of their production to small-scale subcontracting units. This type of employment offered a more flexible work force and could quickly adjust to variation in world demand. In the garment industry, the majority of subcontracted workers are female (about 90%).

Sri Lanka

In the late 1970s, the Sri Lanka government changed its policy from a regulated and inward-oriented economic policy toward one that sought to integrate Sri Lanka into the global economy. The new strategy included: liberalization of imports and foreign exchange; liberalization of the price mechanism and a reduction or even elimination of consumer subsidies; withdrawal of government from direct commercial and production activity; promotion of foreign direct investment; and active encouragement of overseas labor migration. It followed a privatized export-led growth model encouraging export promotion zones, which contributed to an average annual growth rate of more than 5% over the previous two decades. These factors led to a high level of competition for domestic producers.

During this time period, there was a market decrease in the share of agriculture and an increase in the service sector. Contribution of the services sector to GDP growth was 55% of the GDP between 1990–1995. The agricultural sector decreased from over 30% of GDP in 1977 to 20% by 1995. Manufacturing decreased from 23% in 1977 to 15.7% in 1995.

In the early part of the 1990s, surplus agricultural labor looking for alternative employment was drawn into the expanding service sector and the industrial sector. Industrial exports more than doubled in the 1980s and increased a further 85% in the early 1990s. The percentage figures reported in the Central Bank data suggest a decline that could be partly attributed to statistical measurement issues arising from differences in classifying activities. However, there was some decline resulting from the demise of some industries, such as the local textile industry due to foreign competition following the liberalization of trade under the reforms of 1977.

In the early 1990s, there was also an opening up to investment, and the Sri Lanka Board of Investment (BOI) declared the entire country an "investment promotion zone" in 1992. By the end of 1998, over 151 billion rupees were invested in the BOI plan, with over 60% of it foreign. The main sectors targeted for investment were textiles and the apparel industry, which accounted for 16%, and the service sector (including infrastructure projects such as telecommunications, hotels, and apartment complexes), which accounted for 60%.

Competitive pressures from the global market have prompted cost-cutting measures by manufacturers, resulting in the subcontracting of work outside the regulated sector. In addition, stringent labor regulations are also a factor in moving toward flexible labor contracting arrangements.

In terms of the labor force, in 1998 over two-thirds of the employed workforce fell into the non-regulated sector. Only one-third was in regulated employment, protected by labor regulations and a high degree of unionization. Although there was a decrease in unemployment since the change in macroeconomic policy, there still exists a high level of unemployment, and women constitute over 50% of the unemployed workforce. In the garment sector, particularly the export processing zones (EPZ), over 90% of the work force is female. Though women constitute the majority of workers in export processing zones, they are allowed to stay only until they get married. Only 10% of the workforce in the EPZs are married. This is an important factor in determining why women seek employment in the informal sector through subcontracting chains.

India

In 1991, India announced a new economic policy of privatization and export-oriented growth. The main principles of the new policy were: monetary management; budget tightening; exchange rate adjustment; sectoral reforms in fiscal, financial and trade policy; reforms related to the agricultural sector; changing industrial policy; and public enterprise, public administration, and labor market reform (Rana 1997). The industrial policy changes include: delicensing of all but 144 industries in the areas of defense, health, safety, and environment; abolishing the restrictions on the expansion of large businesses; and liberalizing foreign investment regulation. Quantitative restrictions on imports were replaced by tariffs. These tariffs were then reduced in stages from 400% in 1990–91 to 65% in 1994 and to 50% in 1995. The average duty was reduced from 50% to 27% during the same period.

A sharp fall in exports over the two-year period was noticed in pearls, glass and glassware, homeopathic products, and ayurvedic products. This fall in exports was largely offset by an increase in the export of textile items, including cotton and ready-made garments, which increased by approximately 50% and 22% respectively in 1996 97 (Ghutaic 1999).

Development of small-scale industries has been an important objective of the Indian government. This has been facilitated by fiscal concessions in the form of lower excise duties, differential taxation, subsidies, and sales rebates. Easy access to capital markets as well as access to loans and credit have also been part of the reform measures. These and other strategies have had major implications for inter-firm linkages and for the outsourcing of the production process. Closed linkages between small and large firms have been emphasized, and large differences in excise duty charges to the large versus small industries for the same items have made subcontracting thrive in many industries (Pani 1999).

Employment size of the manufacturing industry in India was bi-modal in the 1950s. There was a concentration of workers in either factories employing more than 1,000 workers or in household industries with no hired workers. One of the reasons for the lack of middle range factories was the absence of subcontracting relationships and the vertically integrated nature of manufacturing plants in India (Nagaraj 1999).

There has been a considerable decline in the last four decades in the average size structure of factories, except in the garment sector. There has also been a decline in the number of workers in the household sector and in the factory share of total manufacturing employment. It is therefore assumed that there has been an increase in the non-factory, non-household segment of the manufacturing sector. This assumption is supported by the increase in the share of small-scale enterprises in manufacturing, supported by the new economic policy focus on this sector. Indirect evidence points to an increase in subcontracting units in these small-scale enterprises (Nagaraj 1999).

In the garment industry in the city of Ahmedabad there has been a remarkable growth in the export of India's garment sector beginning in the late 1980s. It grew from U.S. $1,598 million in 1989–90 to $3,675 million in 1995–96. It constitutes 12% of India's merchandise exports and nearly 16% of its manufactured exports.

There are no official estimates of the number of garment manufacturing units or workers in India. A typical garment manufacturer uses smaller units to subcontract out most of the work. The size of these units does not allow them to innovate or to upgrade their products and operations. Yet, the government is promoting small-scale industry in the garment sector. There are no gender-disaggregated macro-level data to measure the gender concentration in this sector. Anecdotal evidence, however, suggests that women are concentrated in those tasks that are less skilled, and that home-based work is primarily done by women.

CONCLUSION

Common to each of the five countries examined has been a move toward an export-led growth model, often assisted by the International Monetary Fund and World Bank structural adjustment programs. The combination of the SAPs, the financial crisis in Asia, and the liberalization of the economy has resulted in an increase in the price of utilities, increased competition with cheap imports, a reduction in subsidies, and an overall need to decrease the costs of production. The specific industries examined experienced a move toward low-paid, low-skilled subcontracted work for women due to push factors, specifically in the case of Pakistan. This preliminary overview demonstrates the need to collect data on outsourcing activity and informal sector employment at both the national and international levels as part of standard macroeconomic data collection. Given the lack of any national statistical evidence on the prevalence of subcontracting and of the involvement of women workers in the process, this chapter is an attempt to gauge these trends through indirect evidence.

In the wake of liberalization, SAPs, and the financial crisis, increasing immiserisation of the labor force—due to privatization/downsizing and poverty—has intensified the distress sale of women's labor. Moreover, the absence of any regulation of the informal sector in general, and of home-based workers in particular, has provided a further incentive to employers to outsource production activity to unorganized women workers under exploitative working conditions. The rise in household expenditures due to macroeconomic changes have led many families to seek extra income by relying on family members who were not previously part of the paid labor force. A large percentage of the women workers in subcontracted labor are new entrants to the labor market. The spatial location of the work is a primary consideration in their decision and ability to seek employment. Many others who were not new to the labor force stayed within the same industry but moved to subcontracting as a result of a factory closing. In Sri Lanka, married women often lost their jobs or were not hired in the export promotion zones because of their marital status. These women turned to sub-contracted work as a way of staying employed. Women working in the industries examined by this study were primarily concentrated in those sectors that are low skilled and where the supply of labor far outweighed the demand. In all five countries, therefore, the women workers were most often relegated to low-wage, insecure marginal employment.

When examining the dual role that women play in both paid and unpaid work, we gave particular attention to those instances where the necessity of performing unpaid work encouraged decisions that countered usual considerations in the wage labor market. The subcontracted work helped bring new entrants into the labor force by spatially locating work in the home. Because their choices were usually limited to subcontracted work or no work, the women often felt that it was better to have low-paid work than none at all. However, all of the workers identified key problems and made strong recommendations on how to improve both the nature and conditions of the work.

Although subcontracted earnings were lower than those offered by formal sector employment, women in general preferred this form of employment because of its flexibility, both in terms of location and in terms of the possibility of working longer hours to earn more money. Women's subordinate position in the family and society made them seek vulnerable positions in order to have greater flexibility. In places where women's public mobility was an issue, subcontracted work allowed for women to earn an income while staying at home. Women's ability to work increased their bargaining position in the household, particularly if they were new entrants into the labor market. There was no real evidence of shared responsibility for unpaid household work. Subcontracted labor seems to reinforce patriarchal notions that women should stay close to home and be responsible for the unpaid care economy (See Chapter 3).

To the women workers, the main problem associated with subcontracted labor is the complete lack of regulation: no consistency in work contracts, difficult working conditions and long work hours, and the difficulty of organizing workers due to their vulnerability and physical location. Workers generally know little about where the products they are producing are sent, in either the domestic or international markets. The process of contracting out work makes it very difficult to hold one employer responsible for protecting workers' rights because of the many links in the chain. The relationship between macroeconomic policy and its consequences on labor conditions needs to be better understood. There is a need not only to collect national-level data to better understand this hidden, yet growing, form of employment, but also to evaluate macroeconomic policy on the basis of its impact on working conditions. Advocacy that promotes workers' rights needs to enhance the bargaining capacity of workers at the local level, to address macroeconomic policies that may threaten their employment opportunities at the national level, and, at the international level, to prevent countries from using cheap labor as their comparative advantage to attract foreign investment.

NOTES

1. The Fordist system of production is characterized by use of assembly lines and task fragmentation.
2. By productivity, we refer to factor productivity of both capital and labor.
3. Especially the "fashion" segment of the apparel commodity chain (Gereffi, 1994).
4. Skill intensity in outsourcing is relative. As Feenstra (1998) states: ". . . outsourced activities are unskilled-labor intensive relative to those in the developed economy, but skilled-labor intensive relative to those in the less developed economy." Thus, skills as well as skill intensity should be seen on a spectrum rather than as an absolute. The only defining criterion must be specific training acquired to undertake a specific task.
5. This will also depend on the formal education intensity of the skill.
6. The "flexible specialization" paradigm is another variant of technological and skill intensive work (Piore and Sabel 1984).
7. The example of computer-aided embroidery in the Philippines case study is one example of this form of subcontracting.
8. Even in continuous flow industries, ancillary activities such as packaging or janitorial services as well as accounting and clerical services are sourced out because of exogenous increase in economic costs.
9. These are goods aimed primarily at the lower income end of the domestic market.
10. For example labor legislation has been an important reason for increasing flexibilization of production in India (Ramaswamy 1999). In Pakistan's case, saving on labor costs through such mechanism is all the more rewarding because small scale/informal sector workers are without legal protection.
11. Though the only direct evidence we show of this is in Pakistan it s common knowledge that the financial crisis in Asia increased poverty levels in Thailand and the Philippines.
12. Interest rates did decline after 1998, but by then bad loans in the banking sector had increased significantly and banks had become increasingly risk averse. High interest rates also resulted in a shift from industrial to finance capital given the incentive structure toward short-termism.
13. Roughly 70% of the State's current expenditure is inelastic, as it is allocated towards defense and debt servicing. Thus, public investment was the only expenditure-reducing mechanism that the state could resort to in order to meet IMF conditionalities.
14. Growth rate of small-scale manufacturing is assumed in National Income Accounts data and has remained constant for two decades now.
15. Even if the producer employs more than 10 workers but is not registered—which is often the case in undocumented economies—the labor laws are not applicable to such industries.
16. While there are still some non-tariff barriers on the import of finished clothing in India and Pakistan, no such barriers exist in the Philippines.
17. See Sayeed and Ali, 1999.

18. The sudden increase in participation rates is, perhaps, due to a change in definition of labor force participation. Otherwise, there is no justification for a sudden rise over a period of four years and then stability again in subsequent years.

19. See Kazi (1999, 390–394)

20. Whether or not the increase in poverty is due to liberalization policies remains a conjectural point. Sayeed and Ghaus (1996), Kemal and Amjad (1997), and Gazdar (1999) draw strong linkages between liberalization policies and the increasing trend of poverty. The argument is based on the simple premise that factors contributing to poverty alleviation in the earlier decades—high economic growth, subsidies on important consumables, high rates of public investment, remittance income, etc.—have been absent in the 1990s. Some factors are absent because of policy reversals and others for exogenous reasons.

21. Whether measured through calorie consumption, head-counts on incomes and expenditures, or a more encompassing basic needs index.

22. See Amjad and Kemal (1997), MHCHD/UNDP (1999), and SPDC (1998).

REFERENCES

Amjad, R. and A.R. Kemal. 1997. Macroeconomic Policies and their Impact on Poverty Alleviation in Pakistan. *Pakistan Development Review*, Vol. 36, No.1.

Applebaum, R. and G. Gereffi. 1994. Power and Profits in the Apparel Commodity Chain. In *Commodity Chains and Global Capitalism*, edited by G. Gereffi and M. Korzeniewicz. Westport: Preager.

Beneria, L. 1999. The Construction of Global Markets: Engendering Polyani's The Great Transformation. *Feminist Economics*, Vol. 5–3.

Beneria, L. and M. Roldan. 1987. *The Cross Roads of Class and Gender: Industrial Homework, Subcontracting, and Household Dynamics in Mexico City*. Chicago: University of Chicago Press.

Diaz, Ma. Eliza O. 1999. Subcontracting and Home-based Work—A Review of Literature. Unpublished manuscript submitted to the Women and Development Program, College of Social Work and Community Development, University of the Philippines, Diliman, Quezon City.

Economic Survey: 1998–99. Islamabad: Economic Advisor's Wing, Ministry of Finance, Government of Pakistan, 1999.

Feenstra, R. 1998. Integration of Trade and Disintegration of Production in the Global Economy. *Journal of Economic Perspectives*, Vol. 12, No. 4.

FOCUS-on-Trade. 1998. Bangkok: *Focus on the Global South* (FOCUS).

Gazdar, H. 1999. Poverty in Pakistan: A Review. In *Fifty Years of Pakistan's Economy*, edited by S. R. Khan. Karachi: Oxford University Press.

Gereffi, G. 1994. The Organization of Buyer-Driven Global Commodity Chains: How U.S. Retailers Shape Overseas Production Networks. In *Commodity Chains and Global Capitalism*, edited by G. Gereffi and M. Korzeniewicz. Westport: Preager.

Ghatate, Vinayak K. 1999. Informal Sector's Contribution to India's Exports: A Quantitative Evaluation. Consultancy project for Self Employed Women's Association (SEWA), Indian Institute of Foreign Trade. Mimeo. New Delhi. March.

Kazi, S. 1999. Gender Inequalities and Development in Pakistan. In *Fifty Years of Pakistan's Economy*, edited by S.R. Khan. Karachi: Oxford University Press.

Kokit, N. 1997. *Unemployed, Broken Family: The Unpredictable Life of the Woman Workers Under the IMF Conditions*. Bangkok: Friends of Women Foundation.

Korzeniewicz, R. and W. Martin. 1994. The Global Distribution of Commodity Chains. In *Commodity Chains and Global Capitalism*, edited by G. Gereffi and M. Korzeniewicz. Westport: Preager.

Mitter, S. 1994. On Organizing in Casualised Work: A Global Overview. In *Dignity and Daily Bread*, edited by Rowbotham and Mitter. London: Routledge.

Nagraj, R. 1999. Sub-contracting as a Means of Technology Diffusion: Evidence from Indian Manufacturing. Mimeo. Mumbai: Indira Gandhi Institute of Development Research. April.

Ong, A. 1997. The Gender Labor Politics of Post Modernity. In *The Politics of Culture in the Shadow of Capital*, edited by Lowe and Lloyd. Durham: Duke University Press.

Pani, Pranab K. 1999. Inter-Firm Linkages: A Study of Small Scale Enterprises. Thesis submitted to the Fellow Programme in Management at the Indian Institute of Management, Ahmedabad.

Piore, M.J. and C.F. Sabel. 1984. *The Second Industrial Divide: Possibilities For Prosperity.* New York: Basic Books.

Profile of Poverty in Pakistan, A. 1999. Islamabad: Mahbub ul Haq Centre for Human Development and the United Nations Development Programme (MHCHD/UNDP).

Ramaswamy, K.V. 1999. The Search for Flexibility in Indian Manufacturing: New Evidences on Outsourcing Activities. *Economic and Political Weekly*, Vol. 34, No. 6; 6 February.

Rana, P.B. 1997. Reforms in Bangladesh: A Comparative Assessment in Relation to Other South Asian Countries. In *The Bangladesh Economy in Transition*, edited by M.G. Quibria. New Delhi: Oxford University Press.

Sayeed, A. and K. Ali. 1999. Labour Market Policies and Institutions: A Framework for Social Policy Dialogue. Study conducted for the ILO. Geneva.

Sayeed, A. and A. Ghaus. 1996. Has Poverty Returned to Pakistan? Mimeo. Karachi: Social Policy and Development Centre (SPDC).

Social Policy and Development Centre (SPDC). 1999. *Social Development in Pakistan*. Karachi: Oxford University Press.

Stigler, G. 1968. The Division of Labour is Limited by the Extent of the Market. Reprinted in G. Stigler, *The Organisation of Industry*. Homewood, Ill.; R. D. Irwin.

United Nations Development Programme (UNDP) Human Development Report. 1997. New York: Oxford University Press.

Standing, G. 1989. Global Feminization through Flexible Labor. *World Development*, Vol. 17, 7.

Williamson, O. 1985. *The Economic Institutions of Capitalism*. New York: The Free Press.

Zaman, A. 1997. *Pakistan: Industry and Trade Sector Study*. Manila: Asian Development Bank.

3

Subcontracted Work and Gender Relations: The Case of Pakistan

Saba Gul Khattak

INTRODUCTION

The definition of the "informal" as opposed to formal sector has been extensively questioned over the past decade as the informal sector has begun to contribute a larger share to national economies. Although worldwide trends indicate an increase in informal sector subcontract work, coupled with a rise in women's and children's share of work in this sector,[1] barely any research studies exist on subcontracted women workers in the Pakistani context.[2] This problem is compounded by the lack of any national level data on the informal sector,[3] and women's work within this sector. The little information that is available is of limited use, as its reliability cannot be gauged. Furthermore, available research reports are based upon micro studies, which lack uniformity in definitional and methodological issues and hence cannot constitute a basis for comparison even within the country. This information does not examine subcontracted work in the wider context of the world economy, either. Usually, the reports look at it in the national context and overlook the links with international structures and the demands of international capital.

A combination of factors has augmented the trend toward subcontracting. The last ten years have seen an increase in subcontracted work as Pakistan's massive budget deficit dictated a reduction in public investment and subsidies and increased indirect taxation. These policy measures were part of the liberalization and privatization policies pursued by the Government of Pakistan under International Monetary Fund (IMF) guidance. According to Asad Sayeed (Khattak and Sayeed 2000, 6–9), various push and pull factors, such as un- and under-employment, technological change, and innovation in organizational strategies to minimize transaction and labor costs or to circumvent labor legislation are responsible for informal sector expansion. The trends in Pakistan indicate that formal sector employment is actually decreasing, with less than 7% of labor unionized, according to the Human Rights Commission of Pakistan Report (1999), and less than 3%, according to the Pakistan Institute of Labor and Research (PILER). Clearly, contract labor and home-based work are taking precedence over formal employment. This is happening because employers are more easily able to evade taxes and to keep overhead and costs of production low.

Furthermore, within the larger national context, we find that the trend toward women's incorporation into the market has increased substantially over the last decade and especially since the introduction of structural adjustment programs (SAPs). Various studies also prove that simultaneously with the introduction of SAPs, especially the liberalization policies, poverty has increased in Pakistan (Sayeed and Ghaus 1996; Amjad and Kemal 1997; Gazdar 1999; Zaidi 1999). Khattak and Sayeed (2000, 18) point out that the increase in poverty in Pakistan has led to an increase in labor supply, especially of women who have never worked before. As firms are pushed into subcontracting, women are expected to sell their labor in distress and take up the lowest paid jobs.[4]

Another major contributing factor to the expansion of the informal sector and specifically home-based work in Pakistan is the lack of legal protection. The government's labor policies and laws have a track record of favoring industrialists and investors (Sayeed and Ali 2000). The government's steadfast refusal to take any measures, even on paper, toward the protection of the informal sector workers is a result not only of the IMF-imposed policies of liberalization and privatization but also of the absence of political will to protect the marginalized. Women and children constitute the bulk of this labor because they are under increasing pressure to supplement the dwindling value of household incomes. They are not only invisible due to their place of work but also rank nowhere on the labor policy priority list.

Although no direct legislation exists to protect home-based workers in Pakistan, international conventions, the constitution of Pakistan, and certain laws—when interpreted broadly—can be applied toward such protection. The existence of these documents, however, does not ensure enforcement. One can assert that Pakistani governments have circumvented labor laws[5] to encourage the marked increase in labor-intensive exports. Additionally, the limitations of legal definitions of employer and employee make women's contribution to the national economy invisible. According to Chen et al. (1999, 607), "Homeworkers represent a fundamental challenge to the inherent challenge of labor law, as they are unsupervised wage employees tied through subcontracts to formal firms." Pakistan's labor legislation and labor data suffers from the same drawback, i.e., it considers workers to be those who are employed in factories with at least ten or more employees. As subcontract work does not appear in the national data on industries, we have no means of finding out how spread-out it is within industries and across the country. For the same reason, we lack information relating to the percentage of women and men within each industry.

The few documents that refer to women's subcontracted work in Pakistan empha-size that it is carried out under extremely exploitative conditions. Due to lack of data, most documents keep referring to the same source—the Pakistan Integrated House-hold Survey (PIHS) of 1990–91. Be that as it may, the Pakistan National Report to the 1995 Fourth World Conference on Women at Beijing (1995, 55), quotes from the said survey, stating that:

> . . . the overwhelming majority of women workers, more than three-fourths of the economically active women in urban areas, are employed in the informal sector. Nearly four-fifths of women in this category work at home as subcontracted labor working on a piece-rate basis, as unpaid family helpers, or as self-employed workers. It is precisely these women who are likely to get excluded from official labor force sta-tistics. . . . These women are confined to working at home, due mainly to cultural restrictions to outside work, which is associated with loss of social status. The lack of job options, the dispersed nature of work, and their pressing need for income limits their bargaining power, making them the lowest paid group, even within the unreg-ulated informal sector.

Echoing somewhat similar concerns, Shahnaz Kazi (1999, 395) writes that, "Women are. . . concentrated in the lowest tiers of the informal economy, employed in casual, unskilled and menial jobs in manufacturing, services and the construction sector."

Such concerns have been surfacing in government documents[6] but little appears to have changed. If anything, women today face worse conditions compared to ten years ago. While the nexus between international economic policies, poverty, and women's incorporation into the labor market has been established to some degree, the linkages between women's empowerment and paid work are also important to explore. It is usu-ally assumed that women's paid work will lead to their independence and autonomy. Is that really the case across the board?

The main points that this chapter aims to underscore relate to the conceptualiza-tion of women's empowerment in the current context. First, there is no automatic tran-sition to empowerment through economic earnings. Thus the assumption that women's incorporation into paid work will necessarily lead to their independence and emanci-pation is flawed, as it conflates women's unpaid labor with the traditional and patri-archal, and their paid work with the modern and emancipated, leading to the notion that once a woman begins to earn money, her status will change. The ability to earn does not automatically mean the relaxation of patriarchal controls. We find that this is seldom the case, as much more (at both the symbolic and material levels) is tied to empowerment and independence than earnings alone. Age, marital status, and class directly impact a woman's level of assertiveness and autonomy. Similarly, the outside environment also needs to be conducive to supporting women. If the social and cultural norms in the surrounding area are women-sensitive, women will not be pushed further back.

Second, the shared conceptions of hierarchies color both men's and women's attitudes. Binary boundaries are maintained and reproduced as they bestow a certain respectability upon women who observe them. Thus the economic gains connected with stepping outside the house might not justify the social censure connected with breaking long-standing taboos. The conception of the good woman who sacrifices in order to feed her family and support her husband during an hour of need by entering an exploitative labor market through home-based work becomes a more acceptable option due to the social consent and approval it sanctions. This is reinforced by factors such as cultural curbs on women's mobility and the inefficient and unfriendly public transport system. Thus low-waged employment keeps women tied to low-status jobs with meager salaries that are much lower than the national per capita income because there is some complicity with the system that ensures that compliance is rewarded. Therefore, one finds that women and men buy into the gender ideology that keeps women in a subordinate position and that there is little incentive for women to challenge gender hierarchies and risk social censure. The absence of any institutional mechanisms that might help women who wish to break out of their subordinate status vis-à-vis their family or the market further promote women workers' exploitation.

Third, women's responsibility for the care economy feeds into gendered divisions of labor. Based on conceptions of women's responsibilities, women's proximity to the home makes them responsible for the care economy, so that the double burden phenomenon transforms itself into a triple burden phenomenon. Even if women are not physically close to their home, they are unable to shed responsibility for the care economy due to entrenched social traditions and ideologies that substitute women's labor (often unpaid) for state responsibility. There is no incentive for governments to change this arrangement, so the lowest paid workers are the ones who are likely to be most exploited because it is hard for them to access either public or private health care facilities. Given their wide ranging responsibilities and an overpowering system that rewards conformity, it is hard for women to think of ways to empower themselves by going against the grain.

Fourth, the view that women's initiatives to organize themselves to fight or bargain for their rights would be successful if they would only self-identify as one category (women workers) in relation to another, antagonistic category (contractors), is a simplistic, dualistic conceptualization. Cross-cutting identities prevent collective action from taking place. The social, cultural, and class affinities that the workers share with the subcontractor prevent them from viewing the latter as the enemy. In fact, they generally perceive him to be a fellow victim of the larger system of exploitation. This compels us to question the conceptualization of the simplistic division between labor and capital. We feel that based on the conflict of interest between labor and the capital class, it would be a simple step to persuade women workers to organize against the contractor.

Such persuasion has not yielded results because, in addition to the unwillingness to risk not getting any work, the supposed animosity among the workers toward the contractor does not exist. It is therefore harder to challenge the system of exploitative levels of wages or devise organizational strategies as the possibility of class conflict is blurred by other layered identities that co-exist with class. Thus the question of women's initiative to be assertive about their work conditions and wages as an indication of empowerment is not a straightforward one, thanks to the complex identities that intersect with women's interests as workers.

METHODOLOGY

This chapter is based upon a survey[7] of 161 workers in three industries, namely, garments, carpets, and plastics, in three Pakistani cities: Karachi, Lahore, and Peshawar. The survey looks at subcontracted work carried out in small factories and at home. We do not count own account work carried out from the home within home-based work. The questionnaire design was based upon the underlying concerns of the study, namely the exploration of the links between macro policies and individual women's lives, their impact on gender relations as well as an exploration of possible advocacy strategies for women workers. The questionnaire was pre-coded to provide quantitative data. Initially a pilot based on approximately 25 questionnaires was tested. Its results were discussed, leading to modifications of the questionnaire. A larger survey of approximately 140 women workers was then initiated in the three cities. Qualitative in-depth interviews with selected respondents have also been used to further explore issues arising from the findings generated by questionnaires. The analyses in this chapter are primarily based upon percentages and figures drawn from questionnaire data gathered from the survey as well as the qualitative interviews.

SUMMARY OF FINDINGS

We conclude that subcontracted work has not brought about any substantial qualitative improvement in the lives of women workers. There might be cases of some increase in women's autonomy, but in general, subcontracted work has contributed to women's exploitation in Pakistan without providing any real empowerment. Subcontracted work has been built upon gender stereotypes and hierarchies that are enforced systematically by the state system, the cultural system, and the demands of international capital.

While we would like to believe that poor women's monetary earnings lead to their empowerment, this has not been the result in a majority of the surveyed cases. These women seldom save for themselves since the level of poverty is intense, and their earnings do not lead to any change in gender relations to their advantage. In fact, they buy into the same ideology that keeps them subordinate instead of questioning it. Our survey findings indicate that a majority of women preferred home-based work despite the knowledge that it entails far less remuneration compared to factory work. Their reasons range from cultural constraints to mobility and language problems as well as the flexibility to combine childcare and household chores with paid work. Does this mean that women workers make autonomous decisions? In this regard, it is pivotal to check for women workers' ability to effectively negotiate their conditions of work and remuneration if they choose to work from the home. They have virtually no bargaining power in the matter, so they become more the victims of circumstance than individuals exercising their autonomy and rights. A majority of the responses from women indicate that they began their first jobs around the time that the negative impact of the structural adjustment program began to be felt in Pakistan. In this sense, they are new entrants into the labor market and are present due to the intensification of poverty rather than due to choice.

While we know that the state is not sympathetic to enacting and enforcing laws to protect subcontracted workers, our survey findings indicate that the awareness of labor laws is extremely low among women workers. There is little interest in finding out more about laws, since most workers find the idea of litigation useless, and any kind of a fight for rights, alien. They view the middleman/subcontractor sympathetically as they perceive him to be tied together with them in a larger system of exploitation. Also, court cases can take a long time to settle, and workers often do not have the incentive or resources to hire a lawyer to fight their case—especially when there is no express law in their favor. Thus, most women workers believe that they cannot rely upon the state and its laws to improve their lot. In fact, barely any perception exists among women workers about state responsibility toward protecting their conditions of work.

The following subsections provide evidence regarding the assertions made above. They give a picture of the work conditions, low remuneration, women's productive and reproductive roles, and the possibilities of organizing for collective action in the overall context of women's empowerment.

Data Profile of Subcontracted Women Workers

This subsection provides a portrait of subcontracted women workers' lives based upon the data generated by our questionnaires. It discusses the major factors that affect these women's everyday existence, such as work conditions, remuneration, and a picture of their household. The purpose is to present specific details about subcontracted women's lives in order to be able to theorize specific contexts and conditions. Our survey data demonstrates that subcontracted women workers have extremely long working hours matched by extremely low rates of remuneration. They have joined the workforce because their families cannot meet expenses due to high inflation and the unemployment of a male family member. Lacking legislative cover, organizational support, and having a weak bargaining position means these women are easily incorporated into exploitative, low paid jobs.

The average age of women workers in our survey is approximately 27 years. The highest percentage (57%) is found in the 20–35 year-old age bracket. The other two age brackets, below 20 and above 35, are almost evenly divided at 21% and 22% respectively (see Table 3.1 for details). Our questionnaires indicate that a large percentage of the surveyed women workers have not worked before, thereby reinforcing the assertion that most have joined work due to economic compulsion (see Table 3.2 for details).

More than half (54%) of the women workers in the survey were literate. It is generally acknowledged that women's literacy impacts their labor force participation. According to the 1981 and 1998 census, literacy among women increased from 37.3% to 56.7%. We can correlate the increase in women's literacy with an increase in women's participation in paid work. However, we cannot correlate it directly with empowerment. The number of years of schooling and quality of schooling are equally important for any assessment of empowerment. It is therefore understandable that despite being literate, women lacked knowledge of laws that might protect them. This probably also has to do with the processes that feed into a lack of support from state institutions—a phenomenon that reinforces the skepticism toward a legal system that remains confined to statute books.

Women workers' working hours indicate that they work at least eight hours daily, six-and-a-half days a week, to meet their work targets (see Tables 3.3 and 3.4). Homeworkers have no medical benefits or social security rights. The women who work in factories stand very little chance of attaining support from the employer in case of a serious injury or illness that requires hospitalization. Seventy-nine percent of the women said they do not receive any medical support for injury at work, while 21% answered in the affirmative. Furthermore, while only 26% of the women workers have access to a government dispensary, 51% said they go to a private doctor in case of illness, while the remaining 23% rely upon a combination of homeopaths, hakims, and government dispensaries.

The average household size is rather large, at 7.66 persons per household. On average there are three earners per household. This average is uniform across industries and cities. The average income of a household over the last six months in all sectors was approximately Rs. 4,500 (approximately U.S. $70) with slight variations across industries (see Table 3.5 for details). Each household has four or five dependents below 14 years of age. We found that roughly 25% of the dependents do not attend school, due to poverty and the fact that the child may be an earner. Given worsening economic trends, this indicates a need for more household members to become wage earners.

This point is also indirectly borne out by the information supplied by many women who said that they were working at their first job and that they had begun working seven years ago—roughly corresponding to the timeframe when the negative impact of structural adjustment policies began to be felt in Pakistan. The average monthly income of women in our survey is Rs. 1,215 (U.S. $22.50), much below the national average of Rs. 1,877 for 1998–99. Women's share of income in total household income is approximately 27% (see Tables 3.6 and 3.7). A majority of the households have contracted loans either for a one-time event, such as a marriage ceremony, illness in the family, or buying a house, or due to an increase in expenditure related to food and groceries. Given this bleak situation, few women retain any savings, especially for personal use (see Tables 3.8 and 3.9).

A substantial number of respondents from all three cities reported that no other women in their family had worked before. The break-down by industry indicates that: 67% of women in the garments sector have no other woman family member who has worked before; 85% of women in the plastics sector reported that no other woman family member has worked before; while 56% of women in the carpets sector have no other women family members who have worked before. This left 33% of women in garments, 15% of women in plastics, and 44% of women in carpets respectively reporting that another woman family member had worked before they joined paid work. Thus, except for the carpets sector, a large majority of women workers had no role models to follow within their own family. To venture into the area of paid employment was not only a new experience for them, but also for the family. One can conjecture that acceptance of this new role has much to do with the economic squeeze that families are faced with.

Conditions Precipitating Women's Incorporation into Subcontracted Work

The attraction of earning an independent wage and thereby acquiring some degree of free will supposedly drives many women to seek employment. Such a desire is taken as a given and we usually build our understanding from this standpoint. However, as stated earlier on, our survey data indicates trends that do not uphold this assertion. This makes the linkage between paid work and free will problematic.

The conditions that induce women to seek paid work relate largely to the macroeconomy and not so much to the internal compulsions/desire of women to work. Additionally, the large size of the family dictates that more money must be brought in, and therefore, women seek employment. This is augmented by the trend of retrenchment in large outfits, which causes a higher percentage of male unemployment.[8] Thus a combination of high inflation, male unemployment, large family sizes, and expenditure increases lead to women's incorporation into subcontracted work.

According to almost 63% of the survey respondents, they have started subcontracted work due to an increase in household expenditures and rising inflation. The death or illness of a family member accounted for 10.31% joining paid work, while 8.25% said that they had started work due to the unemployment of a family member.

Only 8.25% stated that they began working because they wanted to be financially independent (see Table 3.10 for details).

The survey data indicates that structural conditions, rather than the goal of personal empowerment through economic independence, are precipitating women's incorporation into subcontracted work. Concurrently, manufacturers are also happy to subcontract to women, as they can then circumvent labor legislation on minimum wage and working conditions, and thereby lower their costs and maintain flexibility in the quantity of goods they produce. They prefer women workers because they know that women's ability to bargain or retaliate is minimal, due to a range of socio-cultural and structural factors embedded in patriarchy and the economy. In short, worsening conditions fostered by the macroeconomy and pervasive patriarchal controls have led to the particular manner in which women are incorporated into subcontracted work.

Encouragement of Subcontracted Work through Social Conditions and Cultural Norms

Employment, apparently, enables women to help meet the demands of everyday life; however, it simultaneously maintains the status quo and thereby does little to stop the processes of women's subordination. The results derived from questionnaire data show that while traditions and cultural notions of what is appropriate hold women back, economic earnings do not afford them any meaningful autonomy.

The questionnaire data discloses the trends that incline women to seek home-based employment. Some of the questions asked of the women show that cultural norms and traditions play an important part in a woman's decision not to step out of the house. Among the home-based workers, 38% of women reported that they did not seek employment outside the home due to objections from other family members; 33% stated that they themselves considered it wrong to go outside the house; and 23% said that they did not seek work outside the home due to a combination of objections from family members and people in the neighborhood, as well as the fear of creating a bad impression in the neighborhood (see Table 3.11 for details).

A reading of the information derived from the questionnaire reveals that self-censorship plays an important role in limiting women's choices. The opinion of people living in the locality receives relatively low weight compared with that of family members and the women's own opinions, because of the tendency to internalize the social environment and immediately exercise self-censorship. One could call it a defense mechanism: before anyone from the outside objects, the women themselves or their family members impose the codes and restrictions upon their behavior that they are expected to adhere to.

Among those working in factories, 47% preferred to work at home while 53% did not. Opinion among the group that goes out to work therefore appears to be almost evenly divided. This again is a significant finding, indicating that a large majority of the surveyed women prefer to work from home even though the remuneration at home might be significantly less than that at a small factory.

There are two types of plausible explanations for this phenomenon. First, according to Kazi (399, 1999) data from an intensive survey in Karachi (Sathar and Kazi, 1989) indicates that, "Informal employment of women outside the home is also found to have adverse consequences for child survival. The available research based on the Karachi survey indicates deaths were significantly higher for informal sector workers employed outside the home even after controlling for income and education. Informal sector workers were most disadvantaged in terms of child survival, while home-based workers, also belonging to poor households, indicated less of a disadvantage." This evidence indicates that there is some logic to women's preference to staying home. However, the same study also states that children of home-based women workers have fewer chances of attending school compared to those of women working outside the home, thereby proving that in all probability home-based women workers' children are child workers, assisting their mothers in home-based work.

Second, while there is a certain amount of convenience attached to working at home, this convenience is based upon women's gender roles (as the ones with the primary responsibility for the home) and the hostile public arena that discourages women from going outside the home. For example, most women want to avoid using public transport not only because it is inefficient and can take well over an hour to commute one way, but also because they are potentially exposed to sexual harassment. Only two seats are "reserved" for women, right next to the driver of the vehicle (usually a small van or wagon). As these seats are occupied in no time, women, in comparison to men, have to wait much longer before they can catch a van. Sometimes the transporters try to accommodate three women on a seat meant for two persons, thereby making the women feel crammed for space. Women avoid sitting next to the driver because usually his hand, while changing gears, touches the women's knees or legs, which in the local cultural context is tantamount to sexual harassment.[9] Thus, the psychological strain involved in entering the public domain itself is enough to dissuade and discourage women from leaving the house.

The potential threat of sexual harassment also extends to the workplace, where those in management positions can exert power over women workers. There is a widespread perception that due to women's economic vulnerability, they suffer the unwanted advances of men in the factory without being able to put up effective resistance. This perception reinforces the stigma attached to work outside the home. The public arena is thus hostile to women in several subtle as well as direct ways.

Women's Productive and Reproductive Labor

Women incorporate the care economy into their daily work. The double burden phenomenon is now widely recognized with little being done about it. In fact, the negative trends triggered by globalization processes have aggravated this phenomenon further.[10] It has been accepted that human well-being requires more than economic support. The care economy not only encompasses taking care of the sick but also providing emotional and moral support to those who are physically healthy and normal (United Nations Development Programme/UNDP Human Development Report 1999, 78–79). Data from various countries indicate that women spend two-thirds of their working hours on unpaid work (men spend just a fourth), and most of those hours are dedicated to caring work (UNDP Human Development Report 1995). Similar arrangements and outcomes are borne out by the survey data and qualitative interviews conducted for the study.

A snapshot of the life of a woman worker in Peshawar outskirts, Meena, provides an idea of women workers' lives. Meena, like many others, has been working for the last 13 years in a small boutique/tailoring shop. Earlier, she worked from the home (mostly stitching clothes or embroidering). She could not remember the exact number of years she has worked, saying that it seems like "forever." She is the youngest of seven sisters. Ever since she lost her father 25 years ago when she was 13, she has taken care of her ailing mother who decided that her youngest daughter should stay single so as to look after her. A few months ago, when the mother fell extremely ill, Meena's sisters persuaded their mother to agree to Meena's marriage. The unstated logic was that after the mother's death, there would be no one for Meena to live with and a single woman living by herself in a village is socially unacceptable. Meena would need a man's protection and presence in the house; therefore, marriage appeared to be an appropriate solution. The mother agreed, presumably, reluctantly.

By any standards, and particularly by local standards, this is an extremely late marriage for Meena at the age of 38. Meena's responsibilities at the workplace, like her household responsibilities, have increased over the years. They include looking after her mother, cooking, cleaning, and repairing the mud walls of the house during the rainy/monsoon season. Moreover, she is now pregnant. Her income (Rs. 2,500) is insufficient for covering household expenses and her mother's medicines. She has hardly any money left to spend on herself. This has been the pattern all her life. In the past, Meena used to bring home some work to earn additional money; however, this has become virtually impossible at present because her ailing mother demands more attention, and so does her husband. In fact, she showed us some of the quilting work that has been lying incomplete with her for the last six months due to lack of time.

Meena's story is unusual in that she has managed to work outside the house, within the restricted atmosphere of a village on the outskirts of Peshawar. However, due to the care economy, she has had to suffer in terms of a late marriage just so she could continue to look after her mother. In return, her mother will probably leave her the one-room, one-verandah house where they live.

Not only do women workers incorporate the care economy and productive labor into their daily lives; they also pay in other ways: In Meena's case it was her late marriage and late high-risk pregnancy. Quite often women do not get married because they are occupied with bringing home money that helps meet the family's expenses. Thus their work deeply impacts their personal lives. Late marriage or the absence of marriage affects their self-image, as subtly enforced "spinsterhood" is not a phenomenon that is socially rewarded or attractive.

Three other case studies also indicate that women's earnings are crucial to the support of a sick parent or a non-working/jobless husband. For example, Shahjehan is the first of three wives and earns Rs. 1,300 per month sorting plastic and scrap from 8 A.M. to 5 P.M., six days a week. Her workplace is a large plot enclosed by high walls but no ceiling. There is no protection from the summer sun or winter cold. She also shares some of the household work with her daughter and stepdaughters. Her husband was a brick-breaker and general-purpose laborer who stopped working some years ago when his first two wives began to earn money. Both women support him and his third wife. He works occasionally when he feels the remuneration is good.

Similarly, Razia has to support her 70-year-old husband when he comes to visit her for 3–4 months each year, usually during winter. She worries about her 18-year old son who slipped from a roof and broke his right arm. Despite three operations, the arm has become useless, and so his ability to serve customers in the shop he works at is severely impaired. The third case is that of Fokraaj, age 40, whose monthly salary has recently increased from Rs. 1,600 to Rs. 2,000. She stitches children's frocks in addition to supervising and teaching other women in the shop where she works. She is the eldest sibling of two brothers and two sisters. She and her youngest sister are not married. Her brothers are unable to meet the entire amount of household expenses from their electrical repair shop. They say that business is not good, as people these days neither buy electrical gadgets nor bring in the old ones for repair. She said that recently one of her brothers cried because yet another long day had passed without any customer coming to the shop. The brothers were reduced to having green tea (cheaper than black tea due to the absence of milk) with roti (bread) for lunch as they could not afford a proper meal. Fokraaj's income has always been critical for the household. She broke down when she recalled her sick mother's wish to have chicken broth when she could ill-afford to buy a small chicken. She also felt helpless when her mother asked for talcum powder and toothpaste, explaining that despite trying to save by foregoing public transport and walking instead, she was unable to provide more than the doctor's fee and medicines for her mother. She also mentioned that she had managed to save some money in the past for her dowry; however, it was unclear whether she still hoped to get married or was resigned to supporting her family.

While all these women are acutely aware of the centrality of their work and earnings, they are equally conscious of their limitations and helplessness. They feel that compared to their work, their remuneration is unfair. But the needs and survival of the family come first, so they continue to plod through exploitative work conditions and simultaneously shoulder the responsibility of looking after the home, bearing and bringing up children, and looking after sick family members.

Division of Labor within the Household and Help with Subcontracted Work

Given the fact that these women are new entrants in the labor market, we decided to explore whether, and to what extent, sharing of household chores was occurring in order to free up their time for paid work. The purpose was to check for women's double and triple burden phenomenon.

Over 50% of the women reported no change in their household responsibilities after entering the labor market. Some 35–40% reported a decrease in their household responsibilities, while 10–15% reported an actual increase (see Table 3.12 for details). It is not clear what the decrease is related to and who, if anyone, within the household has assumed the extra responsibilities. It is probable that either the grown-up daughters have assumed responsibility for some of the chores, or other women (such as sisters, mothers, or mothers-in-law) have accepted responsibility to support the woman worker. It could also be that the husband and children are helping out.

We do not have specific information in this regard from questionnaire data, as this information was not sought directly. However, the qualitative interviews clearly indicate that household chores as well as home-based subcontracted work involve the labor of children. For example, Salma, who has six children, earns between Rs. 500–700 per month by trimming plastic bottles and cooler caps at home. While the older children work as apprentices in factories for Rs. 100 per week (12–14 hours of daily work, six days a week), an eight year-old son stays at home, as he is too young to be accepted as an apprentice anywhere. He helps his mother with household chores as well as with her paid work. Some women whose daughters were attending school reported that the girls also helped with cooking and washing after school. One can easily conclude that for many mothers, their children are assets in sharing household responsibilities. Women who do not have children, by contrast, reported that they themselves fulfilled the household responsibilities of cooking and cleaning on returning home at the end of the day.

Subcontracted Work, Gender Hierarchies, and New Forms of Power Relations

The induction of women into paid work is expected to raise their status within family hierarchies and accord them more importance. We found that this was not necessarily the case, i.e., there was no automatic correlation between the two. As mentioned earlier on, monetary earnings are important, but not sufficient to bring about a change in gender relations and ideologies.

Some slow-paced social change was detectable, however. Women were accorded more importance within the family as a result of their monetary contribution. Whether this is bringing any immediate change in gender-power relations is questionable, however, since it is based on a non-threatening gender ideology. Some changes in values can be clearly observed, e.g., girls' education receives equal importance; 95% of women said they give equal importance to girls' and boys' education, only 4% said that they give boys' education greater importance, while 1% claimed to give girls' education more importance. Notwithstanding attitudes, as discussed earlier, not all women reported that their children were going to school. A majority whose children do not attend school (roughly 25%) said that they could not afford to send their children to school. In the survey, approximately 53% of boys and 47% of girls attend school. The challenge to gender relations will be very subtle and slow to perceive, since it will extend across generations.

In terms of the importance given to subcontracted women workers' decisions, a majority of women (63%) reported that their opinions and decisions receive importance. Approximately 37% said that their suggestions do not receive importance. There were variations across sectors: 44.64% of the carpet sector women workers said that their suggestions do not receive importance even after the commencement of work; 35% of the women workers in the plastic sector concurred; and only 13% of the women workers in the garments sector said the same.

We should note, however, that despite efforts to sensitize surveyors about the "thrust" of the question, most of the women surveyed interpreted it to include everyday issues, such as what would be cooked in the house or decisions regarding children. It did not extend to the public sphere in terms of decisions related to women's mobility, or more importantly, their own autonomy. For example, none of the respondents felt confident enough to venture outside the existing boundaries of access to the public arena. They did not feel that joining any kind of a neighborhood organization was within the prescribed gender roles. Similarly, staying on until late outside the house in connection with a possible meeting was not an option they could consider without the permission of a male relative or family elder. Thus, one finds that any change in gender relations in women's traditional roles has barely taken place.

Furthermore, it is not entirely clear whether the commencement of work alone determines the importance of decision-making. Decision-making is directly related to marital status in conjunction with the age and status of the woman concerned. If she is older and is a mother or mother-in-law, her say will carry weight. But if she is young and unmarried, she will not be expected to be a part of the decision-making hierarchy. This, of course, implies that the stereotypes upon which gender hierarchies are built are being maintained consciously both by men and women since there is a certain amount of social stigma attached to breaking away. Thus, in order to gain social approbation as well as for reasons of convenience, women will not "rock the boat."

Overall, complaints by men with regard to women's paid work were quite low. Ninety percent of women reported that the men in their families do not object to their paid work. This is probably because the majority works at home, and therefore within the confines of social norms and taboos. Only 7.6% reported household quarrels related to their paid work, while 2.5% admitted that physical violence takes place. This information may have two explanations: first, there may be under-reporting of physical violence for obvious reasons of privacy and pride; second, paid work may not have anything to do with the incidence of domestic violence, which may be caused by a variety of reasons not necessarily connected to structural/economic phenomena.

We also tried to explore whether women felt pressured by their husbands with regard to conjugal relations. The assumption was that after a long day's work, as per cultural and religious presumptions, women might feel it their duty to provide sexual services no matter how tired they were. Not many women were willing to address this issue and those who did stated that there was no conflict with regard to sexual relations.

The low incidence of men's objections to women's paid work is also an indication of changing social attitudes. A somewhat similar survey conducted by PILER ten years ago showed a much higher incidence of objection to paid work. The worsening economic situation in the country has, therefore, forced men to reassess their attitudes about women joining the workforce.

Any change in power relations requires that both men and women change their attitudes. The above information demonstrates that only slow forms of attitudinal change are becoming visible. These attitudes have not been introduced from outside Pakistan, but are rather a result of a combination of factors taking place within Pakistan. However, given the excruciatingly slow pace of social change (and there is no evidence that it will continue in the same direction, as it has been observed to regress in some countries), we can easily conclude that subcontracted work has not provided women with any advantages in power relations vis-à-vis men. If anything, the system of subcontracting appears to have strengthened and reinforced women's subordinate position.

Change in Women's Self-perception

While we maintain that both women and men buy into preconceived notions of gender roles, and that therefore little has changed for women, one can spot the beginnings of a very gradual change in women's lives. It may take generations to reach some semblance of equality. One can optimistically hope, however, that the process has begun.

It is widely believed that women's self-perception and sense of self-worth undergoes a change after they begin to earn money. One may analyze women's self-perceptions in two different contexts: a) personal/private, and b) public. While some change can be observed in the personal context, for example opting for financial independence, the women were at best cautious in the context of the public realm. For example, their reasons for starting work were not only not radical (in terms of seeking a sense of empowerment and autonomy), they were in fact related to the non-threatening stereotyped gender roles of protection and sacrifice for family survival. Similarly, the idea of joining a trade union or a community-based organization was alien to most of them. In the same manner, the idea of attending a meeting of any organization or visiting its offices (even if it was working for their welfare), was equally "iffy", in that it required the permission of the head of the household. Generally, there was a sense of hesitation with regard to issues involving mobility in the public domain. Women's mobility and their physical bodies have enormous representational value in the extremely patriarchal settings in Pakistan. A majority of the respondents, acutely aware of the constraints, did not feel that they had the right to challenge the curbs on their movement or access to institutions.

In our survey, the reasons women had for starting work (as previously discussed) range considerably. Although a majority of reasons pertain to everyday survival, it is important to note that 8% of women opted for financial independence. Mostly, these women were unmarried and wished to pursue work so they might have money of their own to spend as they chose. Furthermore, a relatively larger percentage of women in the plastics sector chose to work in order to acquire financial independence, even though this is not a highly paid sector. It is also a relatively new sector, with 28 being the average age of the women working in it.

We can safely assume that subcontracted work has given a small percentage of women some semblance of financial independence. One cannot overrule the same for the other women even though the reasons for starting work might arise from different compulsions.

While a majority of 69% reported zero savings, some women did acknowledge retaining earnings for personal use. Though we do not know the scope or percentage of income being used for personal use, the fact that such a trend exists indicates that there is a sense of self-worth. It also shows that some women feel that they have a right to spend on themselves after working so hard to earn their money. In this regard, in the garment, carpet, and plastics sectors overall, 39%, 37%, and 51% of the women, respectively, said that they spent a percentage of earnings on themselves. As noted above, a majority of the women who primarily wished to acquire financial independence were employed in the plastics sector. The higher percentage in the plastics sector further strengthens the conjecture that women in the plastics industry also work for themselves and not solely because of family compulsion.

We may thus conclude that women find it easier to assert themselves in the private context, especially in matters that are traditionally within their control or purview, than in the public context, which has traditionally been inaccessible to them. Given this trend, change leading to empowerment in terms of access to resources and control over their own lives is necessarily going to extremely gradual, and spread across generations.

Women's Level of Awareness and Understanding of the Macroeconomy

The level and quality of schooling is crucial for women's understanding of the outside world and the connection between government policies and ordinary people's lives. Awareness of the macroeconomy did not exist among these women, perhaps due to a combination of low levels of education and communication with the outside world. There was a clear sense of being underpaid, but simultaneously there was a sense of coming to terms with reality. As women, they felt that this was the best bargain available to them since they did not have much choice. A repeated response was that if they refused to work at the rates offered by the middleman, he would take the work elsewhere. As a result, they would be unable to earn the little that they were earning. A variation was the belief that given the public arena, they were better off than many others. Therefore, a comparatively low wage for their skills was rationalized on the basis of a Hobbesian world from which they received a bit of protection through the good offices of their employer.

The justification for low wages and exploitative conditions revolved around the issue of limited opportunities and personal choices. The respondents did not associate these issues with structural conditions, i.e., the national economy and the international economic order. Similarly, their knowledge of any legal protection was virtually non-existent. There was rather, in fact, a sense of fatality/predetermination regarding their circumstances. The women knew about factory workers and the advantages accruing to them, but they were acutely aware of their own as well as their employers' (middlemen or saith) limitations.

These findings reinforce the assertion made earlier that cultural and social identities play a critical role in determining the relations between the contractor and workers. Women did not perceive the contractor in a villainous light because of shared class and social background. This of course, has ramifications for any organizing possibilities.

STRATEGIES FOR ORGANIZING

In the course of our research, we felt certain that the women would articulate strategies or steps for resistance. Neither systematically laid-out plans for improving their bargaining position, nor even vague indications about the direction of future planning emerged from the survey, however, as the vast majority of women did not think that they could improve their position vis-à-vis the saith or the middleman who brought them work. This position was related to the cross-cutting class and cultural identities the women shared with the subcontractors, and the fear of losing work and therefore their livelihoods.

Four different questions directed at assessing the possibilities for organizing among subcontracted women workers were included in the questionnaire. Three of these questions were indirect, i.e., they did not ask if the women had any organizing strategies but attempted to extricate this information by asking about related issues. The last question asked directly if, in the woman worker's opinion, she could fight for fairer remuneration through organizing with other women in similar circumstances.

Considering that unemployment of a family member and the rise in expenditures has pushed a majority of women workers into subcontracted work, our first question attempted to explore the degree of friction and competition over trying to obtain work. The results indicate that women do not fight over work. Only 7% reported some degree of fighting or friction while 93% said that they do not fight to obtain or snatch work. This overrules the idea that scarcity sows the seeds of division among workers. In fact, this can be considered a supportive facet for activism to move forward since there is no animosity where work and remuneration is concerned. One may assume that substantial potential for organizing women to defend their interests exists in local communities. However, women have little experience and exposure to community or political organizations.

The second question asked respondents whether they were aware of any kind of organization working on their behalf in their locality. Only 12% answered in the affirmative, while 88% had no knowledge of any such organizing. Again, Peshawar averages are much higher than Lahore and Karachi. The picture becomes substantially more bleak if one removes Peshawar from the scene, reaching a 96% average for the two cities where women are unaware of any kind of organizing in their locality. This makes working with these women all the more imperative but simultaneously all the more difficult, since almost no inroads exist which could be used as a stepping-stone for organizing and strategizing.

The issue of organizing was also explored through a third question about women's personal experiences regarding informal systems of savings. They were asked if they saved any money through the "committee system," in which women pool money, usually on a monthly basis, for a specific number of months. Each month one woman receives the lump sum. Thirty-three percent of the women said that they took part in such schemes, while 67% said they did not. There were some women who did not know what the committee system was, while others explained that there was very little money to save, hence it was impossible to participate. We asked them if such collective solidarity could be extended among women workers with regard to their remuneration. Often, the response was in the negative, though some stated that such a possibility, if it existed, would be ideal. A small number of respondents even tried to explore options, but were mostly unsuccessful. The women did emphasize that they would be interested in working with any organization that might promote such arrangements. The bottom line from our questionnaires and interviews, however, is that no alternative strategies emerged.

Finally, to the question of whether they felt they could obtain a better wage from the employer/middleman by organizing, only 25% of the women replied in the affirmative while 75% thought otherwise. Of the 25%, none were able to discuss concrete strategies to bring this about. Those who responded in the negative explained that the middleman or employer had his own limitations and constraints. They also feared that he would just take the work to another home or community.

Given the fact that only a few women are aware of the possibilities of legal protection (the basis for which are very fragile in Pakistan in any case), and their disadvantage vis-à-vis the subcontractor, there is little room for strategizing at the community level at this point in time. This is not to say that the possibility is nonexistent, but only to indicate that the issue will require a tremendous amount of patience, risk, and painstaking, continuous work within communities and among women workers as well as subcontractors. Simultaneously, and on a more urgent basis, advocacy is required at the national level with policymakers and other stakeholders to provide humane work conditions and fair remuneration to subcontracted workers. This process has already begun, as can be observed in the statements contained in various government reports issued by the labor and women's ministries. These statements must be highlighted and made more public to spread general awareness and force action.

CONCLUSION

The survey data demonstrate that women are joining the workforce due to worsening economic conditions. Their economic contribution to the household is crucial for survival. The fact that they are bringing in an income has contributed very little to any radical change in the position and status within the household or for that matter in the public context. In fact, their relative power position continues to depend upon traditionally drawn parameters and criteria of gender roles to which women themselves adhere diligently. In fact, the larger system of gender relations ensures that there is some degree of convenience to subservience, which is taken as a given by many women.

Capital—local, national, and international—thus colludes with patriarchy to maintain a system that ensures profit by maintaining the gender relations that subordinate women. The case of Pakistan proves that patriarchal controls have not relaxed; in certain instances they have been strengthened to the detriment of women's empowerment. Home-based subcontracted work, just as contract work at factories, has been built up and is thriving due to the usurpation of the rights of workers. A majority of women workers feel that they cannot exercise choices vis-à-vis the conditions of work and remuneration. While male family members do not object to their work, they are not supportive in the sense of proactively helping the women in their work. In the same vein, middlemen and manufacturers are able to keep costs under control and avoid confrontations with labor by distributing work to individual workers in different settings. Where small shops or factories are concerned, workers are prevented from organizing or bargaining because they run the risk of losing their jobs if they do so. Hence, labor regulations are made inapplicable.

Although women's contribution to the national economy is now widely acknowledged and recognized, much of this contribution is taking place outside the formal sector. Women are at the bottom rungs of the informal sector with very few chances of upward mobility. Their own ability to conceptualize and implement alternative strategies that will bring about an improvement in their working conditions, their remuneration, and their level of empowerment in the context of their gender relations is extremely limited.

The lack of legal protection as well as implementation mechanisms compounds the bleak situation further. While it is easy to advocate at the end of research that the affected should organize themselves, we should realize that it is usually quite difficult for those victimized by a particular system to organize against it. In this particular instance, patches of resistance are few and far between. For any useful resistance strategies to be effected, multiple stakeholders need to be involved actively to canvass for improvement in the overall picture. These include civil society institutions such as community-based organizations, non-governmental organizations, the media, and government, as well as international development institutions. Only with concerted action can the negative effects of subcontracted work upon the lives of women workers be reversed.

Women's empowerment will not occur through exploitative work that takes place under unequal structural constraints influenced by pressure from international lending agencies and government policies. Even as an unintended outcome of globalization, the goal of empowerment will take generations to be realized in Pakistan. This is due to the intersection of strongly entrenched patriarchy with global and local capital that dictates that labor be kept in low-waged employment. Since women accept the lowest paid jobs and since there are social taboos upon their mobility as well as other bargaining powers, they suffer the most under this system and continue to remain marginalized and outside of formal sector employment.

TABLES

Table 3.1   Frequency Distribution of Female Workers

Age Group	Percentage
Under 20 Years	21.40
20–35 years	56.60
Over 35 years	22.00
Total %	100.00

Table 3.2A   Percentage Distribution of First Job of Female Workers by City

	Karachi	Lahore	Peshawar	Total %
Yes	56.70	82.00	90.00	75.40
No	43.30	18.00	10.00	25.50
N	60	61	40	161

Table 3.2B   Percentage Distribution of First Job of Female Workers by Sector

	Karachi	Lahore	Peshawar	Total %
Yes	72.50	82.50	67.90	75.40
No	27.50	17.50	32.10	25.50
N	54	57	53	161

Table 3.3   Average Working Days per Week by Sector and City

Sectors	Karachi	Lahore	Peshawar	Average of Sectors
Garments	6.84	6.58	5.70	6.50
Carpets	6.10	6.94	6.80	6.55
Plastics	6.45	5.61	6.08	6.06
Average of City	6.45	6.37	6.18	6.36

Table 3.4   Average Working Hours per Day by Sector and City

Sectors	Karachi	Lahore	Peshawar	Average of Sectors
Garments	9.63	9.55	6.00	8.75
Carpets	7.05	6.48	10.50	7.70
Plastics	7.40	8.20	8.00	7.85
Average of City	8.00	8.04	8.28	8.09

Table 3.5   Average Monthly Income of Household by Sector and City

Sectors	Karachi	Lahore	Peshawar	Average of Sectors
Garments	4005	4726	5717	4691
Carpets	3710	2852	7100	4286
Plastics	4475	3784	6023	4610
Average of City	4058	3772	6335	4520

Table 3.6   Average Monthly Income of Female Workers by Sector and City

Sectors	Karachi	Lahore	Peshawar	Average of Sectors
Garments	700	1564	1907	1323
Carpets	619	474	2899	1224
Plastics	710	1277	1458	1097
Average of City	675	1092	2187	1215

Table 3.7   Average Monthly Expenditure of Household by Sector and City

Sectors	Karachi	Lahore	Peshawar	Average of Sectors
Garments	4082	5013	5383	4776
Carpets	3733	5800	6867	5319
Plastics	4475	3782	5492	4490
Average of City	4091	4916	5975	4881

Table 3.8   Percentage Distribution of Those Who Retain Earnings for Personal Use by Sector and City

Sectors	Karachi	Lahore	Peshawar	Total %
Garments				
Yes				
% Within Sector	20.00	60.00	20.00	100.00
% Within City	21.05	60.00	33.33	39.22
No				
% Within Sector	48.39	25.81	25.81	100.00
% Within City	78.95	40.00	66.67	60.78
Total %	100.00	100.00	100.00	100.00
Carpets				
Yes				
% Within Sector	28.57	19.05	52.38	100.00
% Within City	28.57	19.05	73.33	36.84
No				
% Within Sector	41.67	47.22	11.11	100.00
% Within City	71.43	80.95	26.67	63.16
Total %	100.00	100.00	100.00	100.00
Plastics				
Yes				
% Within Sector	29.63	33.33	37.04	100.00
% Within City	40.00	45.00	76.92	50.94
No				
% Within Sector	46.15	42.31	11.54	100.00
% Within City	60.00	55.00	23.08	49.06
Total %	100.00	100.00	100.00	100.00

Table 3.9 Percentage Distribution of Reasons for Starting Working by City

Reasons	Karachi	Lahore	Peshawar	Total %
Due To Unemployment Of Family Member	21.43	11.11	—	8.25
Due To Death And Illness Of Family Member	14.29	11.11	7.89	10.31
Due To Increase In Expenditure Of Household	35.71	60.00	76.32	62.89
Due To Inflation Only	14.29	6.67	2.63	6.19
Due To Dowry Expenditure Of Sister /Daughter	7.14	4.44	0.00	3.09
Due To Financial Independence	7.14	4.44	13.16	8.25
Separation	—	2.22	—	1.03
Total %	100.00	100.00	100.00	100.00

Table 3.10 Percentage Distribution of Reasons for Not Working Outside the House by City

Reasons	Karachi	Lahore	Peshawar	Total %
Objection From Other Family Members	3.33	46.67	50.00	37.70
Bad Impression In Mohalla	7.14	13.33	—	8.20
Don't Think Its Right	28.57	40.00	50.00	32.79
Objection From Other Family Members and Bad Impression in Mohalla	21.43	—	—	14.75
Objection From Other Family Members and Don't Think Its Right	4.76	—	—	3.28
Bad Impression In Mohalla and Don't Think its Right	4.76	—	—	3.28
Total %	100.00	100.00	100.00	100.00

Note: *Only home-based workers (106 in number)

Table 3.11   Percentage Distribution of Change in Household Responsibilities by City

Responsibilities	Karachi	Lahore	Peshawar	Total %
Grocery Purchasing				
Increase	6.80	18.00	—	9.60
Decrease	22.00	36.10	62.20	36.90
No Change	71.20	45.90	37.80	53.50
Total %	100.00	100.00	100.00	100.00
Cooking				
Increase	1.70	16.40	30.00	14.40
Decrease	25.40	52.50	42.50	40.00
No Change	72.90	31.10	27.50	45.60
Total %	100.00	100.00	100.00	100.0
Dish Washing				
Increase	—	16.40	30.00	13.80
Decrease	23.70	49.20	37.50	36.90
No Change	76.30	34.40	32.50	49.40
Total %	100.00	100.00	100.00	100.00
Washing Clothes				
Increase	—	16.70	27.50	13.20
Decrease	18.60	46.70	40.00	34.60
No Change	81.40	36.70	32.50	52.20
Total %	100.00	100.00	100.00	100.00
Cleaning House				
Increase	1.70	19.70	32.50	16.30
Decrease	20.30	49.20	35.00	35.00
No Change	78.00	31.10	32.50	48.80
Total %	100.00	100.00	100.00	100.00
Upkeep of Children				
Increase	—	25.00	23.70	15.10
Decrease	8.60	51.80	47.40	34.20
No Change	91.40	23.20	28.90	50.70
Total %	100.00	100.00	100.00	100.00

Table 3.11—continued

Responsibilities	Karachi	Lahore	Peshawar	Total %
Children's Education				
Increase	—	22.50	20.60	12.90
Decrease	8.00	47.50	44.10	30.60
No Change	92.00	30.00	35.30	56.50
Total %	100.00	100.00	100.00	100.00
Others				
Increase	—	8.30	17.20	14.30
Decrease	—	58.30	14.00	50.00
No Change	100.00	33.30	10.00	35.70
Total %	100.00	100.00	100.00	100.00

NOTES

1. For example, see Susan Bullock (1994).
2. See for example, Ahmad et al. (no date) whose work relates to the leather industry based on a survey of 800 women workers. Other studies, such as Sabiha Hafeez's (1983), are concerned with the larger issue of women and industrial employment, and do not focus on subcontracted women workers in the informal sector.
3. Out of 70 countries for which the International Labour Organization (ILO) has data, only seven countries had a separate category for homeworkers in their labor force surveys or population census (Chen, Sebstad and O'Connell 1999, 605).
4. Chen, Sebstad and O'Connell (1999, 606) provide evidence from Argentina, Germany, Hong Kong, Italy, Japan, Mexico, and the Philippines that a majority of home workers are women.
5. A review of labor laws in Pakistan related to women and children reveals that all the relevant laws apply to formally registered establishments that hire ten workers or more (see Khan and Khattak, forthcoming, 2001), thereby putting informal sector workers completely outside the purview of law.
6. See for instance the Report of the Task Force of Labour (1994) and the Report of the Commission of Inquiry for Women (1997).
7. This survey and the resultant research was conducted jointly by Saba Khattak and Asad Sayeed (2000) as part of a five-country study on subcontracted women workers, funded by the Asia Foundation.
8. This is due to Pakistan's privatization policy, which dictates that public sector investments and units should no longer be subsidized. Simultaneously, as protective subsidies are withdrawn and taxes levied, large establishments have reduced the number of employees in order to save on production costs. Furthermore, new employment is not being generated. This has added

to unemployment, which, combined with the high inflation rate of the last ten years, has forced most low-income households to enter the informal sector to supplement household incomes.

9. This has come out in various discussions with women workers as well as colleagues. It has also been reported in the press sporadically.

10. This has been documented in detail in the UNDP Human Development Report 1999 (pages 77–83).

REFERENCES

Ahmad, N., S. Qaisrani and M. Tahir, ed. No Date. *Social Protection for Women Workers in the Informal Home-Based Sector in the Leather and Textile Industries.* Lahore: Aurat Foundation.

Amjad, R. and A.R. Kemal. 1997. Macroeconomic Policies and their Impact on Poverty Alleviation in Pakistan. *Pakistan Development Review*, Vol. 36, No. 1.

Bullock, S. 1994. *Women and Work.* London and New Jersey: Zed Books Ltd.

Chen, M. J. Sebstad and L. O'Connell. 1999. Counting the Invisible Workforce: The Case of Homebased Workers. *World Development*, Vol. 27, No. 3.

Economic Survey: 1998–99. 1999. Islamabad: Economic Advisor's Wing, Ministry of Finance, Government of Pakistan.

Gazdar, H. 1999. Poverty in Pakistan: A Review. In *Fifty Years of Pakistan's Economy*, edited by S.R. Khan. Karachi: Oxford University Press.

Human Rights Commission of Pakistan. 1999 *State of Human Rights in 1999.* Lahore: HRCP.

Kazi, S. 1999. Gender Inequalities and Development in Pakistan. In *Fifty Years of Pakistan's Economy*, edited by S.R. Khan. Karachi: Oxford University Press.

Khan, Shahrukh R., and Khattak, S. Forthcoming 2001. Outsourcing of manufacturing to households: subcontracted home-based work by women and children. *Hazardous Home-Based Subcontracted Work: A Study of Multiple Tiered Exploitation.* SPPI Monograph Series. Islamabad.

Khattak, S.G. and A. Sayeed. 2000. Subcontracted Women Workers in the World Economy: The Case of Pakistan, Report of Sustainable Development Policy Institute.

Pakistan National Report to the Fourth World Conference on Women, Beijing. 1995. Islamabad: Ministry of Women, Development and Youth Affairs, Government of Pakistan.

PIHS: Pakistan Integrated Household Survey, Round 2: 1996–1997. 1997. Islamabad: Federal Bureau of Statistics, Government of Pakistan.

PILER (Pakistan Institute for Labor and Economic Research). 1990. Women in the Industrial Labour Force. Karachi: PILER, Unpublished Report.

Report of the Commission of Inquiry for Women. 1997. Islamabad: Ministry of Women Development and Youth Affairs, Government of Pakistan.

Report of the Task Force on Labour. 1994. Islamabad: Ministry of Labour, Manpower and Overseas Pakistanis, Government of Pakistan.

Sabiha, Hafeez. *Women in Industry.* 1983. Islamabad: Women's Division.

Sathur, Z. and Kazi, S. 1989. Female employment and fertility: furthur investigations of an ambivalent relationship. *Pakistan Development Review*, Vol. 28, No. 3.

Sayeed, A. and A. Ghaus. 1996. Has Poverty Returned to Pakistan? Mimeo. Karachi: Social Policy and Development Centre (SPDC).

Sayeed, A. and K. Ali. 2000. *Labour Market Policies and Institutions: A Framework for Social Dialogue*. Karachi: Pakistan Institute for Labour and Economic Research (PILER).

Shaheed, F. and K. Mumtaz. 1990. *Women's Economic Participation in Pakistan: Status Report*. Lahore: Shirkat Gah, and Islamabad: UNICEF Pakistan.

State of Human Rights in 1999. 1999. Lahore: Human Rights Commission of Pakistan.

United Nations Development Programme (UNDP). 1995. *Human Development Report*. New York: Oxford University Press.

United Nations Development Programme (UNDP). 1999. *Human Development Report*. New York: Oxford University Press.

Zaidi, A. 1999. *The New Development Paradigm: Papers on Institutions, NGOs, Gender and Local Government*. Karachi: Oxford University Press.

4

Women Subcontracted Workers in Sri Lanka

Swarna Jayaweera

THE CONTEXT

Subcontracting is an old but relatively invisible mode of production for goods and services in Sri Lanka. It has been a useful mechanism in facilitating labor supply in the plantation sector and construction industry in the nineteenth and early twentieth centuries, and in the early export industries in the 1960s, as well as dispersing production processes in import substitution industries. It began to proliferate in the 1980s and 1990s with the confluence of globalization, the international movement of capital and technology, the international division of labor, the International Monetary Fund (IMF)/World Bank-promoted structural adjustment programs, and the shift in national policy to market liberalization.

The macroeconomic policies introduced at the end of the 1970s gave priority to the removal of the import controls that were characteristic of earlier protection and nationalization policies, and to the promotion of foreign investment and reliance on private sector and export-led growth in order to stimulate economic development (Lakshman 1997). The policy of regional or rural industrialization since the late 1980s has extended the focus of policies beyond the three Export Processing Zones enclaves in operation, increasing the potential for subcontracting island-wide. The industrial policy statements of 1989 and 1995 underscored not only the export orientation of production but also the link between "the large investor and small producer." In the local context, the term "small producer" encompassed the home-based producer. While small- and medium-scale enterprises also resorted to subcontracting to extend their operations, it was the provision of a wide range of incentives to export-oriented enterprises in the liberalized economy that gave momentum to the expansion of subcontracting in the 1990s. In recent years, labor contracts in expanding areas in the services sector have replicated the use of subcontracting as a mode of organizing labor inputs.

The increase in subcontracting as a mode of production in Sri Lanka has clearly been a response to the perceived need by multinationals and local entrepreneurs to outsource or decentralize production processes in order to reduce infrastructural costs, and to use a flexible and peripheral labor force in order to increase profits. Subcontracting's characteristics of minimum capital outlays and low skill-intensive, repetitive labor processes extend the international division of labor from factories to smaller units and home-based production.

While both women and men are subcontracted workers, the majority of participants tend to be women. The increase in the employment of women in subcontracted work is the result of a number of factors. The relatively high incidence of unemployment rates among women, consistently around double those of men over three decades, and the decline and malaise of small local industries since the introduction of structural adjustment programs, has meant fewer options for women in low-income families seeking to generate an income for family survival or upward mobility. The childcare and domestic responsibilities of women in the context of an inequitable gender division of labor within the household limit the mobility that is required for employment in the formal sector. On the demand side, the use of the comparative advantage of low-cost female labor extends from the factory or institutional context to home-based workers.

Despite this expansion, the incidence of subcontracting has been under-reported in studies, (Lakshman et al. 1991; 1994; Dias 1991) largely because its ramifications at the household and individual levels tend to be submerged and invisible. The Subcontracting Exchange Programme established in 1980 was not used by enterprises and was never effective. The Board of Investment regulations require permission to employ subcontracted workers in industries begun with foreign investment, but these regulations appear to be bypassed in practice. As there is no system of registration of contract labor, any quantitative assessment of the size of the female and male labor force employed in subcontracted industries would be unrealistic. Micro-studies, however, have revealed the prevalence of labor contracts and piece-rate processing and assembling at the small unit and home-based level.

Few studies are available in Sri Lanka on subcontracting and on its impact on women. Earlier studies on Export Production Villages captured the experiences of women in assembling inputs in manufacturing industries, agro-based industries, and in agricultural activities (Center for Women's Research (CENWOR) 1988; ITC 1992). CENWOR's pioneering study on the impact of subcontracting in industry on women workers (Jayaweera and Dias 1989) explored their experiences in home-based beedi manufacture, assembling in footwear and the artificial flower industries, and in garment production in small units. The study found that women were at the bottom of a vertical process of subcontracting, without protection of labor laws or trade unions, and vulnerable to the consequences of an inequitable distribution of profits that only benefited entrepreneurs and subcontractors or intermediaries. Studies of women subcontracted workers in other countries have substantiated these findings (Baud 1987; Bhatt 1987; Bhatty 1987; Mitter 1986).

THE STUDY

In 1999 CENWOR participated in a cross-country study of subcontracted women workers, (supported by the Asia Foundation), in five countries—India, Pakistan, the Philippines, Sri Lanka, and Thailand. The study comprised an economist's overview of the economic and labor market context of subcontracting, and a study by the Center of the situation and experience of such women. The study sought to explore the impact of the subcontracting process on the lives of women in general and on their economic and gender roles and relations, more specifically. It further examined the contention that globalization has integrated women into the international labor market on unequal terms.

CENWOR's approach to the study was based on the theory of the interdependence of macroeconomic policies and trends and the ground realities of the economic and social relations of production as they operate at the meso-level of firms and other agencies, and at the level of the social and individual microfoundations of economic behavior in informal units, intermediaries, households, and home-based women producers.

Five areas of subcontracted work were selected, three in export-oriented manufacturing industries—electronics, garments/embroidery and coir—one in agro-based production for the domestic market, and a fifth in the urban construction industry. Efforts to identify suitable samples in the services sector failed and this lacuna is unfortunate.

One hundred and fifty women, 30 in each industry, were interviewed:

1. Women winding coil around a core for use as a component in electronic products, for an electronic factory in the periphery of the Western Province which contracted to produce components for overseas enterprises.

2. Women engaged in embroidery-knitting and smocking for a rural garment factory in the Kurunegala district in the North Western Province, which produces children's wear for a leading overseas firm.

3. Women workers in a traditional "coir village" in the Southern Province, weaving nets and mats of coir and nylon for export by a large Colombo-based firm.

4. Women in a farming community in the agricultural heartland in the North Central Province who cultivate tobacco for a leading tobacco company in the country, and cure the leaves for cigarette manufacture for the domestic market.

5. Women hired by subcontractors for manual labor for construction of buildings at two construction sites in Colombo.

The study included case studies of two women in each industry, and interviews with six men in the families of women workers, two subcontractors in each industry, and key personnel in the firms that subcontracted these economic activities.

Paucity of macro-data and the subjectivity of the responses of entrepreneurs, subcontractors and the women and their families have imposed limitations, but the study findings will hopefully contribute to better understanding of the many facets of policy and practice, and the needs of women workers.

INTERNATIONAL AND LOCAL SUBCONTRACTING

The five selected areas of this study illustrate some of the different manifestations of subcontracting as a production strategy. They underscore the fact that international subcontracting has its local ramifications, as in the garment, coir, and electronic industries, while local subcontracting can take place without international linkages, as in the tobacco and construction industries. International subcontracting was found in the study to have different degrees of complexity and different forms of organization.

In the garment industry, a large overseas retailer firm has established a direct link with a local garment enterprise as an outcome of its global sourcing policy. The firm, however, uses an overseas subcontracting agent to streamline the movement of inputs and exports and to ensure quality control. The Sri Lanka garment enterprise that employs the embroidery workers has ten of its 31 factories (located in two districts) linked exclusively with the main overseas firm. The garment enterprise produces samples in Colombo according to the design and specifications provided by the international subcontracting agent, distributes the approved samples to the appropriate factories for production, and collects the products from the factories at the Colombo site for export. The overseas subcontracting agent takes over the "international" phase and sends the garments to their warehouses for distribution to the retail stores of the main firm, according to its instructions.

The factories are permitted to subcontract to smaller factories at times of peak demand, subject to the approval of the agent's representatives. Strangely enough, the embroidery workers in the villages to whom the factory subcontracts these manual and labor-intensive tasks are not perceived officially as part of the subcontracting process. It is claimed that the work of the embroiderers in informal centers and in their homes is a "value adding" assignment, because the smocked or embroidered product is attached to a garment, and therefore seen as an extension of the work of the factories. The fact that one of the subcontractors is a regular employee of the factory, and is also engaged as a crucial link in the subcontracting chain in terms of supply of inputs, training, quality control, collection of output, and payment of the "external" embroidery workers, lends support to this perception of the garment firm. In actual practice, this categorization or nomenclature appears to be a matter of semantics that obscures the reality of the participation and contribution of the embroidery workers, who are at the bottom of a vertical subcontracting process—outside the "formal sector" in industry.

The major firm, in its document "Global Sourcing Principles," requires all suppliers at different points in the subcontracting chain to ensure that the human rights of their workers are respected regarding such aspects as working hours and conditions, rates of pay, terms of employment, minimum age of employment, health, and safety. All subcontracting units are expected to comply with national labor laws and regulations and to permit employees to join lawful trade unions and other workers' organizations. All production sites are expected to be regularly visited and inspected by the suppliers' agents and by the staff of the main firm. It was observed that the factory which subcontracted the embroidery workers made efforts to comply with these norms and even to provide amenities.

A consequence of the "invisibility" of the embroidery workers in the subcontracting chain, however, is that they operate outside the ambit of these labor regulations. This factory has 16 "centers" managed by 32 subcontractors or "supervisors." The data obtained in the field study clearly shows that minimum wages, statutory working hours, maternity leave, and other workers' rights were not enforced with respect to the embroidery workers as they were in the factory. The inescapable conclusion is that these workers operate in a semi-formal, "grey," or "invisible" area in the subcontracting process, outside the ambit of the global sourcing policy of the main subcontracting firm.

In the coir industry, a large local firm or enterprise has international offices that establish linkages with global sourcing foreign enterprises. This international subcontracting is dependent on subcontracting in the local environment to women workers in the informal sector through women "leaders" of groups who are in actual practice subcontractors. The subcontracting modality used is less involved than in the case of the embroidery garment industry. The local export firm obtains its materials or inputs by (i) purchasing coir twine from the coconut triangle in the North Western Province or the center of the brown fiber industry, and not from the white fiber producers in the South, the location of its subcontracting activities; and (ii) importing nylon rope from two countries in Asia and one in Europe.

These materials are sent in the firm's trucks to the villages identified for location of production. According to the export firm's officials, the leaders of around 700 women groups, identified with some assistance from the Industrial Development Board, collect the materials from the truck and are given specifications of the goods they must produce. The "leaders" are expected to organize the production of coir and nylon netting by home-based women workers. Women leaders hand over the products to the firm's trucks which bring them to the firm in the suburbs of Colombo, where "value adding" takes place by additional manufacturing processes such as "knotting" or weaving the netting. Payment is made to the leaders after months of activity.

The penultimate stage in the subcontracting or international phase is the export by the firm to the United States, Europe, Japan, Australia, and Korea through the offices the firm has established in these countries. These international offices are responsible for finally marketing the products by contacting customers in the countries in which they are located. The products are used for erosion control by central and local government agencies, companies (construction companies in particular), and garden centers in these countries. The Sri Lankan firm is engaged in international operations but is not exclusively tied to a subcontracting enterprise overseas, although its autonomy is limited by the vagaries of the global market. In this sense, it is less overtly dependent than the garment embroidery enterprise.

The term "leaders," or those with whom the firm conducted subcontracting operations, appears to be a euphemism for subcontractors who conform to the established practice of collecting and distributing inputs, collecting and handing over products, and collecting and distributing piece-rate wages. There was no evidence of autonomous groups, participatory organizations, or consensual leadership. The "leaders" were a practical and operational link in the chain between the village and the city.

These leaders were totally unaware of the activities in the chain outside their village. They assumed that the inputs came from a specific country on the basis of identification marks on the polythene bags that contained the materials. They were not aware of the destination of the products. There was no interaction between the firm and the women, and contacts were made via the firm's transport and payment procedures. The firm does not appear to be aware of or overly concerned about the working conditions of the women, or to have intervened to maintain minimum standards.

The women electronic workers were subcontracted by an electronics company that had commenced operations 16 years ago on a small scale in the wake of market liberalization. The company had been a part of an international subcontracting chain importing materials from five overseas firms in two countries to assemble electronic components for what were believed to be finished products finally assembled by the same companies. Its progress appears to have been checkered, as it was wholly dependent on the demands of these firms, and there were occasions when operations ceased. In the early years, according to a CENWOR study on subcontracting in 1989 (Jayaweera and Dias 1989), the women workers worked in the small industrial unit as well as in their homes. With the policy thrust into rural industrialization in the 1990s, the company was able to expand its activities and receive recognition in 1994 as an export-oriented industry by the state Board of Investment. The company has a factory of around 250 workers, mostly women.

The mode of subcontracting has not changed. Materials are sent by the same five overseas companies. Approximately 100 electronic components are being assembled by the company, conforming to the samples and specifications sent by the firms, and the products are then sent by air to these firms. The company is only aware that the products of their labor-intensive operations are inputs into the sophisticated and complex production processes in which the five companies are engaged overseas. The assumption is that these products can be used in the manufacture of products such as cameras, television sets, computers, and circuit boards. The company therefore remains a part of an international subcontracting chain and continues to be at the mercy of market forces, as demand is said to decline annually from November to March for reasons they were unaware of, creating instability and on occasion, even trade union action in the factory.

Production in the factory conforms to the pattern of operation in formal sector factories in the manufacturing sector. The company has also continued to utilize the labor of women seeking to engage in home-based economic activities. This extension of the subcontracting process into the "external" market appears to have also expanded, encompassing many villages in the neighborhood of the factory and in contiguous villages. The subcontractors they employ are former factory employees who have had to opt for home-based activities, as well as other interested individuals. Unlike in the factory, however, the scale of operations has expanded and contracted according to changing demand patterns of the subcontracting companies. The home-based women electronic workers have been therefore more vulnerable to shifting demand in the international division of labor.

According to the data obtained during the study, these women are not protected by labor legislation and their economic activities are characterized by instability and poor returns. They appear to be trapped in the informal or semi-formal sector in the economy at the bottom of the process of international and local subcontracting. They remain officially "invisible" and are described as former factory employees who have been compelled by marriage and childcare responsibilities to be confined to their homes, though able to continue economic activities when there is peak demand for the company's production.

What has emerged from these three areas of study is the relative invisibility of these subcontracted workers in international subcontracting chains in the labor market. It is not surprising that such workers are not "counted" in labor force data or identified in studies that focus on industrial establishments alone. It is apparent that the incidence of subcontracting is much higher than reported in macro, sectoral, and regional studies. It is likely therefore that much of the subcontracting that takes place in the country is unofficial or informal and is cloaked in obscurity. The consequence is that workers in subcontracted industries are left outside the ambit of labor legislation and are particularly vulnerable to the vicissitudes of globalization at the lowest level of the subcontracting process.

The tobacco company included in the study organizes both tobacco growing and manufacture in Sri Lanka, engaging in export-oriented production of tobacco and locally-based production, culminating in cigarette manufacture in Colombo. Subcontracting is confined by the company to local production. The subcontracting chain is well organized with participating units and has been in operation for several decades in the hill country and in the dry zone. The study focused on village-based tobacco growing and processing in a location in the dry zone. The company cooperates with the State Department of Agriculture, which fixes the green tobacco leaf prices before each season, registers the barn owner or subcontractors, and carries out a survey of tobacco cultivation every three years.

Subcontracting operations are organized by the local depot, which started work in 1970 through a group of "barn owners," now numbering about 200. The company provides selected barn owners, who are themselves often cultivators, with inputs such as seeds, fertilizer and insecticides, cash for construction of the barn, and credit through bank loans. Each barn owner is responsible for tobacco from about ten acres of cultivated land. The barn owners or subcontractors, of whom around 5% are women, identify 15–20 women or families in the village who wish to devote the second, or Yala, season to tobacco cultivation, when less water is available for paddy cultivation than in the main (Maha) season. They plant the seeds obtained from the company and distribute the plants, fertilizer, and pesticides to the cultivators according to the extent of land cultivated. The barn owners also assist in preparing the land for cultivation using a tractor and hired labor.

The cultivators tend the plants for around four months and pick the green leaves. The barn owner buys the leaves at the regulated price but reduces the cost of materials and labor supplied. As subcontractors, barn owners are not limited to collecting and buying the village produce and handing it over to the next link in the chain. They have the crucial role of curing or processing the tobacco leaves. The process is carried out in the barn using hired male and female labor and is itself a labor-intensive task. The barn owners take the cured leaves to the company where they are graded, and payment is calculated on rates based on the quality of the products. The company deducts 40% for cost of the material provided for subcontractors and, via them, to the cultivators, and pays the balance, or 60%, to the barn owner/subcontractor. The loan given for construction of the barn is also recovered in installments. Some of the subcontractors are also cultivators and therefore have a second source of income. The local depot deals chiefly with the subcontractors, but its extension staff provides advice on cultivation and ensures quality control. The cured tobacco is sent to the Kandy location of the company for further redrying, processing, and cutting to the required size, and then sent to the company's factories in Colombo for manufacture into cigarettes that are sold in the local market countrywide.

The subcontracting mode is used by the company for cultivation and initial processing of the tobacco leaves, tasks which need to be undertaken at village level. The final processing and manufacture are handled by the company directly, with factory employees in a formal sector enterprise. The subcontracted activities provide the basic inputs into the manufacturing process. Unlike in most enterprises, the subcontractors in the tobacco industry have an enormous and crucial task of not only ensuring the regular supply of inputs for manufacture, but also undertaking the labor intensive task of processing the leaves. They are the link between the company and village cultivators, and, despite the monitoring role of the local depot and the state department, appear to have opportunities to engage in malpractices.

The construction industry has always employed labor at different skill levels. The large companies contract labor to smaller firms, who in turn subcontract labor to meet specific needs—from skilled workers such as masons and carpenters, to unskilled labor. The small establishments organized by individuals have fewer layers of subcontracting as their scale of operations is more limited. They employ their skilled labor directly but subcontract for relatively unskilled tasks such as preparation of concrete slabs.

The women workers in the study were employed in small or large enterprises as unskilled labor at the lowest level. Their specific task was to mix concrete and carry out the initial laying of the concrete slab, a process that is refined and finished by masons.

The subcontracting process begins with a call for estimates for the construction of the concrete slab from around fifteen to twenty subcontractors who generally work with these establishments. The employers select the lowest estimate, and provide the building materials such as cement, sand, and stones to the subcontractor. The subcontractor identifies a group of women and men laborers from low-income families, provides them with equipment and food, and supervises the construction of the slab. Payment to the subcontractor is according to the estimate, and subcontractors pay the workers on the basis of daily wage rates.

The workers are only linked with the subcontractor or, in the case of large enterprises, with the subcontracting small firms. The workers are aware of the final outcome of their labor—the house, hotel, office, or other building—but the different layers of subcontracting in large establishments and even the single layer in the smaller enterprises isolate them from the main enterprise. Subcontracting is, however, a transparent and accepted mode of utilization of labor or labor contract in the construction industry. Daily wage rates tend to be uniform but the working conditions of these workers are determined by market conditions, with working hours extending into the night when required by the pressures of the industry.

It is significant that subcontracting in both local industries (tobacco and construction) is an open process with official approval by the relevant authorities. This official channel or linkage has not, however, benefited women workers who are contracted from the informal sector and are excluded from the benefits stipulated for workers in the formal sector. The study found that the women workers in all five studies shared many of the common disadvantages arising from their indeterminate status in the labor market, whether they were a part of an international or local subcontracting chain. They were also buffeted by the uncertainties of the global market and the impact of macropolicies, which impinged on them all, irrespective of whether the linkages were international or local.

Subcontracting "chains" are not uniform in structure, either, although the underlying principle of expanding production and reducing costs by reaching out to smaller units or to home-based workers and labor in the informal sector underpins all modalities. The findings in this study indicate that it would be more appropriate to speak of levels or layers of subcontracting than simply of chains. Global sourcing for low-cost labor has been the mainspring of international subcontracting. In this process, workers in the formal and informal sectors have been incorporated in the global market as human resources for production, and are vulnerable from a human development perspective.

Four facets of subcontracting have emerged from the study of processes. The invisibility of subcontracted workers operating in a submerged level in the employment hierarchy, particularly in export-oriented industries; the laissez-faire attitudes of many subcontracting firms in the context of the non-recognition of the rights of women workers in the informal sector; instability in the fortunes of both international and local subcontracting firms, which has major implications for the working conditions of women; and the fragmentation of production, such that despite the linkages, the entrepreneurs, subcontractors and workers in the electronic industry, and the subcontractors and workers in the coir industry were not aware of the nature of the final product to which they were contributing inputs.

Role of Subcontractors

An interesting and instructive facet is the role of the subcontractor (male or female) who directly engages the subcontracted workers, and is therefore a lynchpin of the process and a link between the producers and the main entrepreneur or exporter. These subcontractors were used as "external" workers by the enterprises, but wielded considerable authority with the groups of women they "managed." The informal power they enjoyed was reflected in the selection of women workers, allocation of tasks, the monitoring of pace and quality of work, and even in the manipulation of payments and malpractices in the organization of work. Both enterprises and women workers appear to be dependent on their services. The most negative aspect of their participation is that they have garnered a disproportionate share of the profits of subcontracted enterprises relative to the income earned by the women producers on whose labor the subcontracting process in this informal or semi-formal sector depends. It is not surprising, therefore, that some of the women demanded the elimination of the role of these subcontractors from the subcontracting chain.

The role and situation of the subcontracted women workers in the study has to be examined in the context of these structures and linkages.

Women in the Subcontracted Economic Activities

The 150 women workers in the study belonged to families with limited economic resources. The most disadvantaged were the families of the urban construction workers who had a high rate of female and male unemployment. The women were spread over all age groups and the majority were married. All electronic and embroidery workers had some secondary education and nearly 40% had 10 or 12 years of education.

The majority of coir and tobacco workers had some secondary education, and it was only among the urban construction workers that the majority were primary school dropouts. Very few had had any vocational training, and training for their specific tasks had been informal and on-the-job.

The experiences of these women indicate that except in the construction industry, women have found new avenues for generating an income due to the export orientation in the economy in the last two decades, the establishment of garment industries in the rural sector, the spillover of modern industry into villages through subcontracting, and efforts to re-orient traditional occupations such as coir work and agriculture. These opportunities have been crucial in a segment of society in which families are compelled to increase their limited resources through any avenue that is available to them. As the majority are secondary school dropouts with few opportunities for vocational training, their access to more remunerative employment in the formal sector has been limited. The minority of those with a complete secondary education has also been constrained by the high incidence of unemployment in the country.

Throughout the study, economic imperatives have emerged as the decisive factor in seeking employment. The fact that the majority of women were married and a small number were single parents may have determined the opting of employment in home-based economic activities. One-third had been employed previously, chiefly in the formal sector. One-half of these women had worked in garment and other factories, service sector jobs, trade and domestic service, but not in other subcontracted work. Many of them had been compelled by childcare and household responsibilities to change to their current employment. Others had transport difficulties, inadequate remuneration, or had lost their jobs. In this context, and given their circumstances, the majority of the women perceived subcontracted industries as a more beneficial and practical alternative to regular employment.

The work experiences of these women underscore the characteristics of a modality that straddles the formal and informal sectors, using intermediaries chiefly from the workers' environment to make a relatively organized link between large-scale formal enterprises seeking to expand production and largely home-based women workers. The construction industry, for example, is a typical urban informal sector economic activity that uses the labor inputs of poverty groups for arduous manual operations.

Working Conditions and Economic Returns

The women in this study were "out workers", engaged in monotonous labor-intensive tasks that served as inputs into a larger production process. They were engaged for these tasks by subcontractors assigned by the enterprise. The coir, tobacco, and construction workers did not receive any training, but the electronic and embroidery workers were "trained" in these specific tasks by the subcontractors. The electronic and coir workers carried out their tasks in their homes, the embroidery workers in an informal village center and in their homes, the tobacco growers in their own fields, and the construction workers on building sites. With the exception of the construction workers, these workers were physically isolated from the main local enterprise that subcontracted them.

The information provided by the women on their working conditions underscores their vulnerability in a production system that operates outside the formal sector. Only half the women had continuous work while the rest faced instability, reflecting the relative fortunes of the enterprises and the demand for their products, as well as fluctuations in the construction industry. Tobacco workers had seasonal employment and were the only group that had another economic activity—assisting in paddy cultivation on their family plots during the main season. Working hours depended on the exigencies of demand and consequent pressures to meet production targets, and were not limited by labor regulations (see Table 4.1). Nearly 40% had to be assisted by their husbands, children, parents and siblings to meet targets (see Table 4.2). They had no respite to perform their biological reproductive role, necessitating their temporary withdrawal from economic activity and hence a loss of income related to childbirth.

Payment to the electronics, embroidery, and coir workers was made on the basis of piece-rates per specified number of units. Payment for tobacco growers was based on output per season. Construction workers were paid daily wage rates. Economic returns from participation in these subcontracted industries were relatively poor. Two-thirds of the construction workers said that they were unable to compute their monthly income. Of the remaining women workers, 95% earned below Rs.2500, the minimum wage stipulated by the State for the formal sector at the time of the study. The 5% who earned above this level received Rs.2500 to Rs.3500 (see Table 4.3). The economic returns of these women workers were not commensurate with their arduous labor inputs, and job instability further reduced their incomes. Nonetheless, participation in subcontracted industries was the livelihood for the majority.

Approximately half of these women articulated their grievances regarding instability in employment, inadequate wages, irregularity in payment of wages, absence of social security benefits, and the arbitrary actions of subcontractors who were perceived by some to be the major beneficiaries of the subcontracting process. Employment in subcontracting industries was, however, seen as a necessity in order to meet basic family needs. Most work-related problems appeared to stem from the exclusion of these workers from the ambit of labor legislation.

Overall, these women are at the bottom of a production system from which they have received minimal economic rewards and benefits commensurate with their labor inputs. The situation, however, was not uniform in all the study locations. The embroidery workers appeared to have the best working conditions, being "out workers" in an enterprise that has attempted to "look after" the workers in the factories. But they were also vulnerable to the inbuilt flaws of subcontracting as a mode of production. Electronics, coir, and tobacco workers were clearly at the mercy of subcontractors and the more "remote" authority of the main enterprise. The construction workers were unskilled labor employed in heavy work.

The case studies provided insight into other facets of the impact of work in these industries. There was, for example, concern that the fertility of the soil would be adversely affected by tobacco cultivation. Occupational health problems were also a matter of concern. An electronics worker for instance, said that she had neck pains and tearing eyes and that her eyesight was failing as a consequence of intensive concentration on winding coils. A coir worker said that her elbow was swollen and her fingers injured by the rough coir. She had hand, arms, shoulder, and chest pains caused by tying the bundle in the knot in the coir net. She had to take two painkillers a day, and in fact had been medically advised to stop working for some time. Such experiences point to the negative impact of these economic activities, but they are apt to be overlooked by workers in favor of the immediate need to generate an income. As with other forms of labor-intensive employment, the long-term health effects related to subcontracting work are not well understood.

GENDER ROLES AND RELATIONS IN THE HOUSEHOLD

It is not possible to establish direct relationships between women's work in these economic activities and their domestic roles and situation, but four aspects investigated could be indicative of trends: (a) contribution to household income; (b) division of labor in the household; (c) participation in decision-making in the household; and (d) attitudes of family members to women's participation in these economic activities and status in the family.

Women's economic role has been strengthened as a result of their participation in economic activities. Only 12.7% of the spouses of these women earned between Rs.3,000 and Rs.5,000 a month and 7.3% between Rs.5,000 and Rs.8,000, chiefly in the families of electronics workers. Mean household monthly incomes ranged from Rs.1,914 (tobacco growers), Rs.3,614 (coir), Rs.4,712 (construction), and Rs.4,966 (embroidery) to Rs.5,654 (electronics). According to their own estimation, only 39% of the households could live within their incomes. Minimum incomes were Rs.200 (construction), Rs.625 (coir), Rs.1,600 (embroidery), Rs.2,000 (electronics), and Rs.2,200 (tobacco). One-third of the households had no savings, though two-thirds had not taken loans. Consequently, most women belonged to families who either were below the "poverty line" or would be below it if the women had not engaged in these industries. Earnings from subcontracted work were estimated to range from 40% to 75% in households with income less than Rs.2500, and to decrease with a rise in household incomes (see Table 4.4).

The contribution by the women workers may have made the difference between absolute poverty and some economic stability in families either struggling for survival, seeking escape from poverty, or aspiring to upward mobility. Some of the women said that they were able to use a part of the income they earned to send their children to private tuition, implying that their contribution was also directed to promoting upward mobility through the advancement of their children's employment opportunities. The majority of spouses and other family members clearly appreciated the benefits accruing from the economic participation of these women. The major cause of dissatisfaction was the meager remuneration they received.

The pattern of sharing domestic tasks was also explored in regard to 14 specific tasks comprising household chores, childcare in the case of women with children, and external activities such as marketing. The task which 72.4% of the women said they had to cope with largely alone was care of the sick. Around 40% to 50% of married women had no assistance in childcare and 30% to 50% of the women bore the sole responsibility for household chores. There appeared to be some form of sharing of household tasks in at least half the households. The participation of husbands was highest in marketing (30%). There was minimal participation in washing plates and cooking utensils (6%), care of the sick (4.7%) and sweeping the house (4.3%)—tasks usually viewed as "feminine." Share participation in other household tasks and childcare was between 10% and 18%.

The traditional inequitable gender division of labor appears to have changed very little in the context of home-based economic activities, which perhaps reinforces inequality. While the home-based workers had the advantage of some flexibility denied to women who are full-time workers outside their homes, in reality their working day, comprised of both economic and domestic tasks, extended over just as many hours. Assistance from extended family in rural and low-income urban families and the help of children has enabled women to cope with domestic and economic roles, but with a cost— reflected in the long hours of work and the use of family labor, particularly child labor.

Responses regarding decision-making in the household revealed both expected and unexpected facets. Parents, for example, were found to be the decision-makers in the families of unmarried women workers. These women form the majority of embroidery workers, are few in number among electronics, coir, and tobacco workers, and are almost nonexistent among construction workers. In this study, parental authority and the norm of a patriarchal head of household continues to be strong in rural families irrespective of whether daughters are income earners or dependents. This situation would perhaps have been different if the young women had worked away from home, as studies of women workers in Export Processing Zones and in overseas domestic employment have indicated. Among married women there was no perception of male dominance in any of the areas explored in the study, from daily activities to children's education, health care in the family, economic decisions, and use of leisure time and excursions. The pattern of power-sharing appeared to be one of joint decision-making by the spouses in many families.

According to 62.7% of the women, their decision-making powers had increased with their economic activity. They reported that they had the freedom to buy what they wanted to, spend more—including on the private tuition of their children—save more, invest, and go on pilgrimages. They felt they were better able to make decisions for the family. Such economic empowerment appears to have taken place primarily among the electronics, embroidery, and coir workers. From the pattern of decision-making that emerged from the study, it appears that the tobacco growers and construction workers already enjoyed such power and that there was no significant change in their situation.

Economic participation also reportedly increased the self-confidence of 70% of the women workers. Two major reasons were articulated: having their own economic resources meant they were no longer dependent on spouses or family to spend or save as they wished; and confidence that they could "run the family alone" led to more acceptance of their views within the family. A lesser proportion (50.7%) felt that their self-esteem had increased. Tobacco growers, for example, saw themselves as undertaking an identifiable activity and making an individual contribution, in contrast to their traditional role as agricultural producers participating in a family enterprise that subsumed their contribution in a family income (see Table 4.5).

While participation in subcontracted industries was seen as an economic imperative, only a minority of the women (26.4%) felt that their participation had increased the respect of their spouses.

Perceptions of the Status of Subcontracted Women Workers in Society

Only 38% women workers believed that their economic activities had enhanced their status in the community. A higher percentage (64.6%) felt that they were accepted in society as income earners as a consequence of their greater economic resources and their ability to participate in community work. These women made a distinction between recognition of their economic position as income earners and their social status in the community. Social status is clearly a more complex issue and is dependent on the "level" in the occupational hierarchy. The fact that these women, despite being economically empowered, have perceived no improvement in their societal position in either their own estimation or in the estimation of the community, is a reflection of the poor quality of the employment they are engaged in.

Subcontracting as Compared with Regular Employment in the Formal Sector

A crucial issue explored in the study was whether or not women workers perceived the subcontracted industries in which they participated as more beneficial or advantageous than regular formal sector employment. A substantial majority of women workers (76%) said that it was more beneficial, while over half (53.3%) said that working in their own home was an advantage because there was no need to incur expenditure on "good clothes" or on transportation to and from work. Some construction workers said that payment on a daily basis was convenient as it met their immediate needs. Those who preferred regular employment emphasized that subcontracting wages were low, employment was not permanent or "respectable," no increments were given, and there was no fixed day for payment as in the formal sector. In the perceptions of this minority, however, practical considerations outweighed this negative assessment of their subcontracted work.

Views of Men in the Families of Women Workers

The views of the men in the families of women workers substantiate many of the responses of women. Subcontracted work was their last preference in type of employment but they welcomed the economic participation of women as a source of income in their resourceless families. Few had negative perceptions of the impact of these economic activities on the well-being of their families: only 15.3% felt that it negatively affected household work; 13.3% felt it negatively affected childcare; 20% said it negatively affected family life; and 13.3% said it negatively affected family relationships. Their estimation of their own participation in household chores and in decision-making was more positive than that of the women but there was no evidence of overt male dominance in gender relations in these aspects of family life. The men, however, were far more overtly critical than the women of the inequities they perceived in an economic system that uses women as low-cost labor without adequate economic and social returns. They complained in particular about inadequate remuneration, unstable employment, absence of benefits such as maternity benefits, and the occupational health hazards of these jobs.

Trends and Issues

The study found that macroeconomic policies in the last two decades have promoted subcontracting as a mode of production. The study also substantiated the findings of earlier studies that economic imperatives have pushed women in low-income families into these income-earning activities, and that consequently, women have had access to new employment opportunities and to a degree of economic empowerment, despite their vulnerability at the bottom of a system of production.

While subcontracting is not a new mode of production, the increasing involvement of overseas firms, including multinationals, since the liberalization of the economy, has both directly and with local collaboration created the phenomenon of international subcontracting. The chains or levels of such subcontracting extend beyond factories in the formal sector to small units and home-based individual production in the amorphous informal sector.

In the absence of comprehensive quantitative data it is not possible to estimate the contribution of subcontracting to total production. This mode of production has, however, clearly facilitated economic development by expanding production beyond the limits of formal enterprises, which in the perception of entrepreneurs, are constrained by infrastructural costs.

The benefits to the national economy are, however, limited by the fact that factory enterprises and subcontracting in manufacturing industries are often only found in assembly-type operations. The import content of inputs is consequently high, as quantitative and qualitative problems in the delivery of local inputs and relative costs (as perceived by entrepreneurs) prevent the development of backward linkages in the national economy. This study found that the highest local input came from the dependence of the tobacco industry on its interventions in local agriculture.

While globalization has stimulated the expansion of subcontracting, the uncertainties of the global market introduced a marked element of instability in the fortunes of both large-scale international firms as well as local establishments. Such vicissitudes occurred independently of national policies, and they remained an issue of concern in the context of the need for sustained economic development and livelihoods.

In a competitive, profit-oriented market with increasing fragmentation of production, subcontracting is likely to expand further at different levels of production, drawing more home-based women workers into its operations.

It is vital that the subcontracting process and its outcomes be assessed in terms of labor issues and social and human rights criteria. The study findings have reinforced the concerns articulated in earlier studies regarding the use of the labor inputs of women to increase production and profits without commensurate returns with respect to economic rewards and related benefits. The use of women as low-cost labor units in industries in the formal sector has been documented extensively. The same process without any regulatory framework has taken place in the informal sector with often less visible links between the industrial establishments and the submerged contracted workers in the flexible "external" market. Women workers in both categories have been incorporated in this process in the international labor market on unequal terms.

The pressure from employers for the degradation and consideration of labor, such as the demand to modify the Termination of Employment Act to enable flexibility in hiring and firing practices, is reflected already in macro data in labor force surveys. The demand for a flexible supply of labor is likely to increase, resulting in the movement of some labor from regulated to unregulated employment, and in the concomitant expansion of the relatively invisible semi-formal subcontracting sector stretching across the formal and informal sectors.

Labor legislation in Sri Lanka conforms in general to international standards and has a relatively long history. Enforcement, however, has tended to be weak, as can be seen in the debate on overtime and in the denial of the right to association in Export

Processing Zones. Subcontracted workers are even more disadvantaged as they are outside the orbit of labor regulations and their working conditions tend to be a non-issue for policy makers, administrators, and trade unions. On the other hand, Sri Lanka did ratify the International Covenant on Economic, Social, and Cultural Rights and the United Nations Convention on the Elimination of All Forms of Discrimination against Women (CEDAW) in 1993, as well as the domestic Women's Charter of 1993, all of which spell out the rights of workers, including in the informal sector. It has failed as yet to promulgate the domestic Workers' Charter formulated a few years ago, however. None of the international instruments, local policy formulations, overt stances of some overseas firms on ensuring labor rights, or the highly vocal human rights discourse has had an evident impact on the working conditions of subcontracted women workers.

Women subcontracted workers are likely to increase in numbers in response to continuing "push" factors in the socioeconomic environment. While the overall incidence of unemployment has declined in the last few years, the unemployment rates of women have been consistently double those of men. Poverty and its multi-faceted dimensions continue to haunt around 30% of the population. This study found that women subcontracted workers made a substantial contribution to family income and to family survival, maintenance, and upward mobility through investment of their incomes in the education of their children. In the Sri Lankan context, these women are also part of a labor reserve of relatively educated women with nine to twelve years of education, as advertised in the brochures of the Board of Investment. They have benefited from the provision of free education over five decades but the lack of alternative opportunities compels them to seek employment as subcontracted workers. It has to be noted, too, that subcontracted industries offer income-earning opportunities for women who are less physically mobile—women who need to combine childcare and economic activities within the confines of their homes or informally in the vicinity, in the context of the gender ideology that universally underpins household work. Consequently, they respond readily to the demand for labor in such despised enterprises. Their objections relate to the role of intermediaries, and the lack of adequate wages and workers' benefits.

This study and others has indicated that engaging in economic activities affects prevailing patterns of gender roles and relations. Women subcontracted workers are economic producers irrespective of whether they are counted in labor force surveys. The economic empowerment many have gained through control of the economic resources they generate, and their own perceptions of increased decision-making power have contributed to change in some facets of gender relations in the family. The location of their economic activities in the home, however, appears to have reinforced the inequitable gender division of labor in the household.

In the context of the present and prospective trends in the expansion of subcontracted industries, the findings of the study underscore the need for change at both policy and operational levels from human and national development perspectives. The women workers and the men in their families have identified two scenarios of change:

1. They proposed expansion in subcontracted work, as they considered their economic participation in these activities to be crucial to the survival and maintenance of their families. There was the proviso, however, that working conditions should concomitantly improve. Suggestions included the availability of uninterrupted work or permanent employment, regulations and letters of appointment, better payment and facilities such as social security, bonuses, medical allowances, provision of food, tea, and drinking water, compensation for occupational health hazards, day care centers and resource centers for the purchase of materials and sale of products. In fact, these suggestions are consonant with working conditions in the formal sector and with provisions in labor legislation, and go even beyond them.

2. Some of the women proposed an alternative, so as to bypass the subcontractors, who in their view, increase the production costs of enterprises and reduce their remuneration. Enterprises, they argue, could deal directly with women's groups through their nominated or elected representatives and could also assist in setting up resource centers for the purchase of the materials and payment for products— that is, subcontracting without subcontractors.

It is not certain that enterprises will intervene to improve their working environment and conditions significantly, although the overt policies of overseas companies have set standards for all international and local subcontractors. Eventually, the State needs to intervene to protect the human rights of its citizens. The Board of Investment, for example, which has already laid down some regulations, must publicize them and monitor their implementation. The enforcement of labor laws is weak and should be strengthened and extended to support subcontracted workers as the Wages Board Ordinance is said to cover production in subcontracted economic activities. Sri Lanka should also be urged to ratify the new International Labor Organization's (ILO) Convention on Home-based Workers, which protects the rights of workers like those captured in this study, and to ensure that labor legislation is consonant with the provisions of the International Covenant on Economic, Social, and Cultural Rights, and the CEDAW.

Regarding the alternative modality proposed that enterprises should deal directly with women's groups—non-governmental organizations (NGOs), women's organizations and even State programs such as the Integrated Rural Development Programs/Regional Economic Advancement Programs—need to facilitate the mobilization of strong and cohesive women's groups and promote linkages with enterprises. No

NGO has intervened directly thus far to assist these women, although legal literacy programs are conducted on the community level. It will not be an impossible task, however, in view of Sri Lanka's history of two decades of social mobilization and "change-agents" programs and the skills and experience already developed in organizations and communities.

Over the years, self-employment projects have been promoted and implemented within the frameworks of "Women and Development", "Credit and Savings," or "Poverty Alleviation." They have not contributed significantly in assisting low-income families to move out of poverty, because they have provided credit without including critical inputs such as technology, vocational and management skills, quality control, and marketing information. In addition, macropolicies have been biased against micro-enterprises (Jayaweera 1996). If the State provides adequate incentives for small independent producers, and if economically viable projects are organized in small units by the relevant agencies with these inputs, women in low-income families seeking a means of livelihood (like the women in this study) will have an alternative mode of generating an income, which will enable them to also develop autonomy and self-respect.

The major task is to prevent the social exclusion of women in low-income families and their marginalization in poorly remunerated, dead-end jobs in vulnerable working conditions. The macroeconomic policy framework should meet their needs as much as they satisfy the requirements of large-scale entrepreneurs and investors. Some safeguards also need to be introduced at international (United Nations), regional, and sub-regional (the South Asian Association for Regional Cooperation/SAARC, for example), levels.

Women's groups, activists, and academics have an important role in undertaking policy and action-oriented research, particularly to monitor the situation of women in subcontracted industries. The findings of such research need to be used to develop purposeful advocacy programs for policy change at the national level, to improve working conditions, assist women in mobilizing themselves to engage in economic activities with enterprises, and to protect and promote their interests and rights.

Note: This chapter is drawn from CENWOR's study "Invisible Women: Workers in Subcontracted Industries in Sri Lanka." Study Series No.15.

TABLES

Table 4.1   Working Hours/Day

Working Hours/day	Electronics		Embroidery		Coir		Tobacco		Construction		Total	
	No.	%	No.	%	No.	%	No.	%	No.	%	No.	%
1–2 hours	5	16.7	—	—	4	13.3	—	—	—	—	9	6.0
3–4 hours	19	63.3	—	—	11	36.7	1	3.3	—	—	31	20.7
5–6 hours	6	20.0	—	—	4	13.3	10	33.3	—	—	20	13.3
7–8 hours	—	—	1	3.3	5	16.7	19	63.3	3	10.0	28	18.7
9–10 hours	—	—	2	6.7	5	16.7	—	—	1	3.3	8	5.3
11–12 hours	—	—	15	50.0	1	3.3	—	—	1	3.3	17	11.3
13–14 hours	—	—	11	36.7	—	—	—	—	2	6.7	13	8.7
No fixed hours according to work	—	—	—	—	—	—	—	—	22	73.3	22	14.7
No response	—	—	1	3.3	—	—	—	—	1	3.3	2	1.3
Total	30	100	30	100	30	100	30	100	30	100	150	100

Table 4.2   Assistance from Household Members in Subcontracted Work

Assistance	Electronics		Embroidery		Coir		Tobacco		Construction		Total	
	No.	%	No.	%	No.	%	No.	%	No.	%	No.	%
No help	17	56.7	30	100.0	16	53.3	1	3.3	30	100.0	94	62.7
Husband	6	20.0	—	—	1	3.3	9	30.0	—	—	21	14.0
Daughter	2	6.7	—	—	2	6.7	2	—	—	—	6	—
Son	—	—	—	—	—	—	1	—	—	—	1	0.7
Husband & Children	—	—	—	—	2	6.7	13	43.3	—	—	15	10.0
Mother	2	6.7	—	—	2	6.7	—	—	—	—	4	2.7
Parents	—	—	—	—	1	3.3	1	3.3	—	—	2	1.3
Sister	—	—	—	—	2	6.7	—	—	—	—	2	1.3
Brother	2	6.7	—	—	—	—	—	—	—	—	2	1.3
Mother-in-law	—	—	—	—	1	3.3	—	—	—	—	1	0.7
Sister-in-law	—	—	—	—	—	—	3	10.0	—	—	3	2.0
No response	1	3.3	—	—	3	10.0	—	—	—	—	4	2.7
Total	30	100	30	100	30	100	30	100	30	100	150	100

Table 4.3   Monthly Income from Subcontracted work

Monthly Income	Electronics		Embroidery		Coir		Tobacco		Construction		Total	
	No.	%	No.	%	No.	%	No.	%	No.	%	No.	%
< Rs.300	—	—	—	—	4	13.3	—	—	—	—	4	2.7
Rs.300-< Rs.600	9	30.0	—	—	4	13.3	7	23.3	—	—	20	13.3
Rs.600-<Rs.1000	8	26.7	1	3.3	2	6.7	9	30.0	—	—	20	13.3
Rs.1000-<Rs.1500	13	43.3	5	16.7	0	30.0	9	30.0	5	16.7	41	27.3
Rs.1500-<Rs.2000	—	—	15	50.0	2	6.7	1	3.3	3	10.0	21	14.0
Rs.2000-<Rs.2500	—	—	4	13.3	4	13.3	1	3.3	—	—	9	6.0
Rs.2500-<Rs.3000	—	—	1	3.7	1	3.3	1	3.3	—	—	3	2.0
Rs.3000-Rs.3500	—	—	3	10.0	—	—	—	—	—	—	3	2.0
No Response	—	—	1	3.7	4	13.3	2	6.7	22	73.3	29	19.3
Total	30	100	30	100	30	100	30	100	30	100	150	100

Table 4.4   Percentage Contribution of Earnings From Subcontracted Work to Household Income

Household Income (Rs.)	Electronics		Embroidery		Coir		Tobacco		Construction	
	No.	%	No.	%	No.	%	No.	%	No.	%
<2,500	1	75.0	3	64.9	6	40.5	1	50.0	7	57.9
2,500-<3,500	5	22.8	3	64.7	10	28.0	8	21.1	5	46.0
3,500-<5,000	8	17.9	10	41.2	10	30.4	15	21.0	1	40.5
5,000-7,500	8	12.3	10	30.4	2	34.8	10	17.3	—	—
7,500-10,000	7	10.6	2	33.3	—	—	1	13.5	—	—
10,000 & above	1	8.3	2	20.8	1	4.2	—	—	—	—
Total	30	14.1	30	35.3	29*	27.1	30	19.5	13**	49.2

*One worker did not report her income

**Information with respect of 17 workers were either not reported or was found unreliable

Table 4.5 Perceptions of Women Workers

Perceptions	Electronics		Embroidery		Coir		Tobacco		Construction		Total	
	No.	%	No.	%	No.	%	No.	%	No.	%	No.	%
Increase in Respect from husband*	14	53.8 N=26	4	36.4 N=11	6	28.6 N=21	0	0.0 N=24	3	16.7 N=18	27	26.4 N=102
Decision-making power	27	90.0	21	66.7	19	63.3	14	46.7	14	46.7	95	63.3
Self-Confidence	30	100.0	13	43.3	22	73.3	27	90.0	14	46.7	106	70.7
Self-esteem	13	43.3	10	33.3	14	46.7	27	90.0	12	40.0	76	50.7
Higher status in community	9	30.0	5	16.7	10	33.3	20	66.7	13	43.3	57	38.0
Better accepted by society as income earners	24	80.0	7	23.7	22	73.3	27	90.0	17	56.7	97	64.7
More benefit than regular job	28	93.3	22	73.3	23	76.7	26	86.7	15	50.0	114	76.0
Improvement in position of women as income earners as a result of economic development	25	83.3	28	93.3	24	80.0	26	86.7	10	33.3	113	76.3
Total	30		30		30		30		30		150	

*Percentages based on number of Married Women (N)

REFERENCES

Baud, I. 1987. Industrial Subcontracting: The Effects of the Putting Out Systems on Poor Working Women in India. In *Invisible Hands*, edited by Andrea Menefee Singh and Anita Kelles, Chapter 5. New Delhi: Vitanen Sage.

Bhatt, E. 1987. The Invisibility of Home-based Work: The Case of Piece-rate Workers in India. In *Invisible Hands*, edited by Andrea Menefee Singh and Anita Kelles. New Delhi: Vitanen Sage.

Bhatty, Z. 1987. Economic Contribution of Women to the Household Budget: A Case of the Beedi Industry. In *Invisible Hands*, edited by Andrea Menefee Singh and Anita Kelles, Chapter 6. New Delhi: Vitanen Sage.

Dias, S. 1991. Subcontracting in Small-scale Industries, the case of Sri Lanka. In *Industry and Development*, No. 29.

Export Production Villages. 1988. Study Series No. 2. Colombo: Center for Women's Research (CENWOR).

Export Production Villages—A Study of a Sri Lankan Scheme for Rural Export Development. 1992. Geneva: ITC.

Jayaweera, S. 1996. Facets Affecting Women's Entrepreneurship in Small and Cottage Industries in Sri Lanka. New Delhi: ILO-SAAT.

Jayaweera, S. and D. Malsiri. 1989. Subcontracting in Industry: Impact on Women. London: Commonwealth Secretariat.

Lakshman W.D. et al. 1991. Changes in the Industrial Structure and the role of Small and Medium Industries in Developing Countries: The Case of Sri Lanka. Tokyo: Institute of Development Economics.

Lakshman W.D. et al. 1994. *Small and Medium Industry in an Intermediate City—A Case Study of Kurunegala in Sri Lanka.* Colombo: Karunaratne and Sons Ltd.

Lakshman W.D. et al. 1997. Introduction. *In Dilemmas of Development.* Chapter 1. Colombo: Sri Lanka Association of Economists.

Ministry of Women's Affairs. 1993. Women's Charter of Sri Lanka. Colombo: Sri Lanka Government Press.

Mitter, S. 1986. *Common Fate, Common Bond—Women in the Global Economy.* London: Pluto Press.

5

THE VIEW FROM BELOW: Impact of the Financial Crisis on Subcontracted Workers in The Philippines

Rosalinda Pineda Ofreneo, Joseph Y. Lim and Lourdes Abad Gula

The Philippine economy has been buffeted by the winds of globalization, and affected quite severely by the Asian financial crisis of 1997 and 1998, from which it has not recovered. Although subcontracting has been endemic in manufacturing and even in agricultural industries as a way of saving on labor costs, and therefore maintaining competitiveness in both the local and export markets, there are indications in some areas of a decrease in subcontracted home-based employment due to the adverse impact of trade liberalization. This trend is more dramatic in the garments industry, which has experienced a marked deceleration in growth since the mid-1990s, and has undergone restructuring that has led to less subcontracted work being offered to traditional embroidery communities. The employment of labor-saving, computer-aided embroidery machines in garments factories has worsened the situation. What remains of subcontracted work at the home-based level is extremely low-paying and time-consuming. Subcontracted homeworkers organized under the Pambansang Taga-pag-ugnay ng mga Manggagawa sa Bahay—National Network of Homeworkers (PATAMABA)—are therefore confronted with the reality of disappearing and progressively less rewarding employment. Through participatory action research, they have been able to grasp their particular situation more concretely and with a holistic perspective, and suggest sustainable courses of action within a broader empowerment agenda.

This paper will examine the impact of the financial crisis in Asia by focusing on the garment industry. The macroeconomic changes brought about by a series of free trade agreements has had serious consequences for the garment industry and the scope of subcontracting in that industry. Using the results of the study conducted in 1998, this paper examines the program and policy implications by looking at the experience of PATAMABA, an NGO working with women workers. Finally this paper links the effect of macroeconomic changes to the organizing efforts at the local level.

THE GENDER EMPLOYMENT PATTERN IN THE 1990S

The Philippine employment pattern for men and women in the 1990s saw a virtual closing of the gap in unemployment rates between women and men. Table 5.1 shows that from an unemployment rate of 10.28% for females and 7.3% for males in 1989, the gap between these two rates continuously narrowed in the 1990s to the point where in 1999, when the Philippines was still being affected by the Asian financial crisis, the unemployment rate for males became marginally higher than females (9.47% for males versus 9.19% for females).

The closing of the gap is not due to an increase in female employment in manufacturing (as happened in the 1970s and 1980s). In fact, female employment rates in manufacturing and agriculture (where most tradable goods production is located) consistently declined during most of the 1990s. The sectors that consistently absorbed female labor in the 1990s were the service sector (especially after 1993), the wholesale and retail trade sector, and the finance sector (all non-tradable sectors).

This picture emerged in the 1990s because of increasing competition from imports, due especially to tariff reduction and overvalued currency during the pre-crisis 1990s. Thus the growth period in the 1990s brought higher production in the non-tradable goods sector (services, wholesale/retail trade, transportation, construction, and finance), than in the tradable goods sector (mainly manufacturing and agriculture which were facing stiff competition from imports).

During the Asian financial crisis (1998-99), manufacturing and construction were major losers, and employment absorbers remained in the services and wholesale/retail trade sectors. Since these sectors were more female-oriented, the 1990s as a whole favored employment absorption of females, but in the informal, unprotected, low wage, and low productivity sectors.

One of the biggest losers in the manufacturing sector during the mid-to-late 1990s was the garment sector, which is the biggest employer of females in the manufacturing sector and the biggest employer of subcontracting activities.

THE GARMENT SECTOR

The garment sector is the biggest employer of home-based subcontracted women. It is a troubled sector. This became clear in 1996 when it registered a sharp decline of almost 9%, coinciding with the start of the decline in garment exports. From then on, the share of garments in total manufacturing stagnated between 5.5% and 5.8% from 1996 to 1998. At the same time, the share of garment exports in total exports declined sharply from almost 22% in the early 1990s to just 8% in 1998.

The even more pronounced decline of the textile sector started earlier. After registering strong growth between 1987 and 1989, textile output started to decline throughout the entire 1990s, from 4% of total manufacturing in the second half of the

Table 5.1   Employed Persons by Major Industry Group and Sex: October Figures (as % of labor force)

FEMALE	1987	1989	1991	1993	1995	1996	1997	1998
Total employed	89.11	89.72	89.52	90.02	90.58	91.83	91.54	90.15
Unemployed	10.89	10.28	10.48	9.98	9.42	8.17	8.46	9.85
Agriculture, Fishery and Forestry	29.15	27.74	26.92	29.40	28.15	27.80	25.97	24.63
Mining and Quarrying	0.13	0.18	0.13	0.11	0.08	0.12	0.10	0.05
Manufacturing	11.22	12.18	11.89	11.36	11.51	11.06	11.08	10.26
Elec., Gas and Water	0.14	0.19	0.16	0.16	0.17	0.14	0.18	0.18
Construction	0.19	0.17	0.25	0.22	0.19	0.19	0.31	0.26
Wholesale & Retail Trade	22.00	22.61	23.04	22.54	23.57	23.94	23.88	23.94
Transportation, Storage and Communication	0.58	0.59	0.50	0.60	0.66	0.70	0.82	0.89
Financing, Insurance, Real Estate and Business Services	1.65	1.68	1.83	1.99	2.06	2.35	2.43	2.44
Community, Social and Personal Services	24.04	24.35	24.80	23.60	24.11	25.53	26.78	27.48
MALE	**1987**	**1989**	**1991**	**1993**	**1995**	**1996**	**1997**	**1998**
Total Employed	91.93	92.70	91.90	91.79	92.28	93.05	92.51	90.48
Unemployed	8.07	7.30	8.10	8.21	7.72	6.95	7.49	9.52
Agriculture, Fishery and Forestry	51.84	49.28	49.56	49.03	47.70	45.07	44.01	42.93
Mining and Quarrying	0.94	0.92	0.87	0.71	0.50	0.55	0.60	0.50
Manufacturing	7.69	8.14	8.06	7.84	7.77	8.26	7.90	7.59
Elec., Gas and Water	0.48	0.45	0.53	0.53	0.48	0.58	0.63	0.61
Construction	5.15	5.97	6.43	6.41	6.95	8.34	8.52	7.59
Wholesale & Retail Trade	6.90	7.17	6.44	6.93	7.25	7.63	7.92	7.74
Transportation, Storage and Communication	6.22	6.94	6.87	7.70	8.10	8.49	8.89	9.12
Financing, Insurance, Real Estate and Business Services	1.70	1.66	1.76	1.77	1.91	2.26	2.14	2.09
Community, Social and Personal Services	11.01	12.12	11.34	10.81	11.56	11.84	11.88	12.29

Source: Labor Force Survey, National Statistics Office

1980s to only 2.3% in 1998. Textiles were never a significant export of the Philippines, with textile share of total exports declining from 1.2% in the early and mid-1990s to 0.8% in 1998.

The decline of the textile sector was a big blow to the garment sector. An integrated garment-textile industry would have given garment exports a boost with higher value-added and efficiency gains in overhead, transportation, and vertical integration. As it was, most raw materials and intermediate goods for garment exports had to be imported.

The employment share of garments and textiles in total manufacturing was much higher than their contribution to gross value-added. Data from the Bureau of Labor and Employment Statistics (BLES) showed that garments comprised 17.5% of total manufacturing employment in 1988, declining to 15% in 1998. Textiles, on the other hand, comprised 7.9% of manufacturing employment in 1988, declining to 5.6% in 1998.

The garment industry is the second largest employer in manufacturing (after food), while the textile industry is the fourth largest (after electrical machinery and apparatus). (The statistics grossly underestimate the number of people employed in the garment industry, as only formal establishments employing ten workers and above are surveyed. They do not reflect employment in firms with less than ten workers, or firms and workers in the informal sector, including home-based workers.) The Garments and Textile Export Board (GTEB) estimates that there are close to a million workers in the garment industry if all the subcontracted and homeworkers are included.

During and after the recession of 1991, real wages declined sharply and continuously for the garment and textile sectors. This was likely caused by sharp inflation in the early 1990s (especially in 1991) and by strong competition from foreign goods resulting from trade liberalization, tariff reduction, and overvaluation of the currency. A further explanation for the sharp and continuous fall of real wages in the garment sector during the period from 1996 to 1998, was that employment in the sector kept rising while garment production and exports steadily slowed down. This indicated a possible oversupply of labor in garments geared for the domestic market.

The strong labor-intensive export promotion strategy undertaken by the Marcos government in the 1970s, spurred partly by attractive incentives for foreign investments, changed the composition of Philippine exports. Instead of being largely agricultural and resource-based, exports shifted to non-traditional manufactured exports, concentrated on garments and related products as well as semiconductors and electronic parts. Since both the garment and electronic industries were heavily dependent on female labor in the final assembly stage of production, this increased the female labor force in manufacturing. Production in these two export areas, however, was import-intensive. This yielded low value-added since intermediate products such as electronic parts and textile fabrics were largely imported from abroad.

The promotion of these two sectors led to a significant rise in subcontracting. More firms and individuals accepted subcontracted work to supply the demand of exporting firms. Production of semiconductor and electronic exports was largely firm-based (either directly by export firms or by subcontracting firms) while production of garments was more flexible, allowing for a combination of both firm-based and home-based production. From the 1970s to the mid-1990s, the formalization of many garment firms led to a significant amount of subcontracting to home-based workers (garment production traditionally had a large pool of home-based workers). This practice spread not only in garments but also in many non-traditional export areas such as leather products, footwear, toys, handicrafts, housewares, non-traditional agricultural products, and livestock and poultry—areas where home-based work already had a high incidence. Unfortunately, regular economic and labor statistics do not capture the extent of subcontracting in both firm and home-based production. Only formal subcontracting firms are being monitored and no regular data on the number of subcontracted workers are available.

By 1996, as shown by some statistics on the top products of the Philippines, it is apparent who the winners and losers are in terms of growth rate and export share. Among the big winners are electronic and electrical equipment and parts (including semiconductors), and machinery and transport equipment. These products, however, have the highest import content among export products and yield low value-added unless backward linkaging is achieved. The dependence of exports solely on semiconductor and other electronic parts is especially disturbing, as they comprise almost 60% of total dollar export earnings.

Among the clear losers are garments, footwear, wood manufacture, baby carriages, toys, games and sporting goods, basketwork, wickerwork and other articles of plaiting materials, and miscellaneous manufactured articles (including *papier-mâché*). Unfortunately these are precisely the sectors where many women home-based and subcontracted workers are employed. This explains why, in the communities studied, subcontracting work for export products has declined enormously. Garment exports, in particular, have stagnated to the extent that their share of exports fell from 21.7% of the total in 1990 to a mere 8% in 1998. They were replaced by machinery and transport equipment as the second top export earner (after semiconductors and electronic parts) starting in 1997.

Significantly, the 1990s were a period of intense competition in world export markets. Import intensity grew as import liberalization and tariff reduction intensified. In the mid-1990s, the increasing import intensity became more pronounced and even harmful as domestic monetary policies of the Central Bank before the Asian financial crisis favored the inflow of volatile short-term capital to prop a stable and overvalued exchange rate. This further cheapened imported products and made Philippine export products expensive in the world market. It not only reduced the competitiveness of many Philippine export items and increased the import intensity of the country, but also unnecessarily intensified foreign goods competition with Philippine tradable products, mostly in manufacturing. This reduced the attractiveness of the manufacturing sector and shifted many investments to the non-tradable sector (e.g., real estate, financial institutions, wholesale and retail trade, and private services). In turn, this precipitated the now well-known Asian financial crisis. Meanwhile, garments geared for the domestic market at present face stiff competition from imported products from China and South and Southeast Asia, which now have lower tariffs and can easily enter the domestic market.

The Asian financial crisis came just as job orders and piece- (and pay) rates were declining for many of the home-based subcontracted workers engaged in the manufacture of garments, handicrafts, footwear, toys, baskets and plaiting, and other miscellaneous products. The Asian financial crisis in 1998 and 1999 had two dimensions: the financial and economic crisis that hit basically urban areas, throwing workers out of manufacturing, construction, finance, and real estate; and the El Niño/La Niña phenomena, which increased unemployment and underemployment in the agricultural and rural areas.

PROBLEMS OF THE GARMENT INDUSTRY

The causes of the problems facing the garment sector can be classified into external and domestic causes. Of the external causes, four cry out for attention and circumspection, namely: world trade; the lifting of quotas; the North American Free Trade Area (NAFTA) and Caribbean Basin Initiative (CBI); and the growing competition with imported goods.

First, world trade, involving the World Trade Organization (WTO), the Asia-Pacific Economic Cooperation (APEC), the ASEAN Free Trade Area (AFTA), and NAFTA, has increased the participation of China, India, Bangladesh, Sri Lanka, Indonesia, Mexico, the Caribbean Basin countries, and the Eastern European countries in the export of low-cost garments. Many of these countries have a huge labor surplus and/or are increasing their efficiency. Thus they can pay low wages and charge low prices for their export products. They have indeed taken a significant chunk of the export market of garments from the Philippines.

Second, the lifting of quotas under the Multi-Fiber Agreement of the WTO negotiations is detrimental to the Philippines, as it enjoys a favored status in the United States and European Economic Community (EEC) markets. In fact, the decline in garment exports in 1996 was partly a result of the initial phase-out of quotas as exports in the main U.S. market fell that year. That the United States is trying to circumvent the lifting of quotas to favor its own garment manufacturers further complicates the problem. For instance, in July 1996, the United States changed its rules of origin such that the place where a piece of garment is produced is no longer considered to be where it is cut, but rather where the most important assembly (e.g., textile production) occurs. What this implies is that the Philippines could lose its quota for garment and made-up textile products since these can only be considered made in the Philippines if the textile fabrics are sourced locally. Considering that the Philippine textile industry is underdeveloped, what could be more detrimental than upsetting sourcing patterns and confusing quota arrangements?

Another important implication of the lifting of quotas is that Philippine garment exports, which are of mediocre quality by world standards and used only as a secondary source for garments, will be in jeopardy. There is no need to mention Hong Kong and China, which are now constrained to limit their garment exports.

Third, NAFTA and the CBI are giving Mexico and Caribbean garments and other exports destined for the U.S. market an unfair advantage, to the detriment of Philippine garment exports whose main destination is the U.S. market.

Fourth, there is growing competition with imported products for garment production geared to the domestic market. Import data from the National Statistics Office (NSO) show that imports of textile yarn, fabrics, and made-up articles (the latter being an intermediate garment product) have grown quite fast in the 1991–97 period of globalization, reaching almost $1 billion in 1997. Final garment products are also increasing at a fast pace (from $13 million in 1990 to $65 million in 1997) although they are coming from a very low base.

Apart from the four external causes just probed, there are, on the other hand, at least five domestic reasons for the garment sector's problems, such as: (1) high labor costs relative to world standards due to historically high inflation rates and higher cost of living, as well as lower productivity; (2) higher electricity costs and poor infrastructure; (3) labor problems hitting large garments exporting firms (Aris, the top garment export producer in the Philippines, closed down in 1996 due to labor problems. During the same year, the other two top export producers, Gelmart and Novelty, also reduced their production because of labor problems. Another top exporting firm, Midas, declared bankruptcy as a result of debt problems due to the financial crisis and some labor problems in 1998. Labor problems expectedly arose as management's way of coping with intense foreign competition usually at the expense of labor); (4) overvaluation of the peso from the mid-1980s up to 1997, which made exports expensive abroad and cheapened imports domestically; and (5) low investments in efficient and productive machines by the big firms. This last reason no doubt is associated with the boom-bust cycles (which reduce business confidence), high interest costs (due to International Monetary Fund (IMF) monetarist policies that make lumpy investments expensive), and periodic credit crunches in the Philippines.

One response to the garment sector's problems, within the framework of the globalized world, is to address the domestic causes of the loss of competitiveness. Another is to diversify to other countries away from the over-concentration on the U.S. market, as well as find niches in export products in which the Philippines has comparative advantage. One possible niche is the production of high value-added and high technology garment products in the high-end of the fashion industry. The latter has yielded some relative gains. This explains the continuing success of some garment-exporting firms. But diversifying away from the U.S. market has so far not been successful, especially in the context of the Asian financial crisis.

A NEW DIMENSION OF SUBCONTRACTING

In general, subcontracting is defined by the International Labour Organization (ILO) as "an industrial or commercial practice whereby the party placing the contract requests another enterprise or establishment (the subcontractor) to manufacture or process parts of the whole of a product or products that it sells as its own." More specifically, international subcontracting is defined in terms of "all export sales of articles which are ordered in advance and where the giver of the order arranges the marketing."

Because wages are a key determinant in the competition for global markets, transnational corporations (TNCs) set up branches or subsidiaries in the so-called "low-wage countries" or joint ventures with local entrepreneurs. Later, the TNCs encouraged growth in the developing states of supplier or subcontracting firms, which may be branches and subsidiaries of the TNCs themselves, joint ventures, or "independent" producers. Still, these supplier or subcontracting firms were dependent on the contractor corporations. They performed the ancillary role of either processing the materials supplied by the latter or manufacturing or assembling the components. To TNCs, the advantage of international subcontracting is that it reduces their visibility in terms of direct equity investments while they still retain control through the market and their monopoly of technology.

Domestic subcontractors can either be independent or subordinate. Whereas the latter is dependent on one large customer that buys almost all of its output, the former has access to more than one buyer.

The intense foreign competition in the export and domestic markets has given subcontracting a new dimension. Subcontracting and related practices have become potential coping mechanisms of firms, due to noncompetitive labor costs (a result of previous high inflation rates that had led to high costs of living), labor-management conflicts (especially in garment, textile, chemical, and pharmaceutical plants), and flexible firm size (to improve efficiency). At the same time, however, home-based subcontracting seems to have shrunk as traditional sectors (especially the garment sector) employing these workers have stagnated or have substituted machines and/or computers for labor (such as in embroidery).

Subcontracting in the Philippines is now multi-level. Orders come from a foreign principal in the United States, Japan, Australia, or Europe. The Manila-based exporter then subcontracts the work to provincial manufacturers or agents, who in turn farm out the jobs to rural households. The foreign principals, the exporters/suppliers, and the big subcontractors can bring down production costs to a minimum, principally through cheaper labor and lower capital requirements. They also have maximum flexibility because they can increase or decrease production depending on fluctuations in demand. When demand is high, workers can be made to produce more. When low, they can be made to produce less or none at all.

According to Donald Dee, President of the Confederation of Garments Exporters in the Philippines (CONGEP), there has been a change in marketing layers. In the past, small or big U.S. stores ordered their supplies indirectly through importers, who then would develop supplier or subcontracting firms in the Philippines. The trend today is for U.S. superstores like K-Mart to bypass importers and to buy directly from manufacturers in the Philippines. Unlike importers, who are buying only for themselves, these direct buyers do not give volume orders but have more requirements. They cancel orders as they choose, and demand shorter production periods.

There has also been a shift in local production arrangements because of these developments. Previously, importers opened up markets and were able to choose quantities. They could decide on the kind of garments to be imported from, say, the United States, and could give volume production to manufacturers in the Philippines. They could also give orders a year ahead of the season, thus assuring manufacturers of continuous business. With the shift to direct buying, big exporters have shifted from subcontracting via a contractor to "direct subcontracting." They now contract several smaller producers, provide them with machines, advance the payroll, etc., in exchange for exclusive use, multi-skilling, flexibility in work arrangements, better quality control, and assurance of dependable delivery. These "direct subcontractors" can be likened to departments or branches of a big exporter firm, except that they shoulder their overhead, apart from machines and labor.

In any case, subcontracting is inevitable in the Philippine garment industry. Big contractors sometimes evolve into big exporters, but contractors as a separate class are a vanishing breed. There are indications that such contractors are now paid to train the workers that their satellites are going to use. In effect, they have become employment agencies for subcontracted garment workers.

The number of subcontractors accredited by the Garments and Textile Export Board (GTEB) decreased from 2,396 in 1993 to 1,502 in 1997. In-plant workers employed by subcontractors decreased from 121,690 in 1993 to 100,270 in 1996. Homeworkers decreased from 5,126 to 2,381 in the same period. Employment figures improved in 1997, with in-plant workers numbering 159,033 and homeworkers, 2,546. Subcontractors are still concentrated in Metro Manila, Southern, and Central Luzon.

There was a rapid decline of employment in 1998, although the number of accredited subcontractors increased by five to 1,507. In-plant workers employed by subcontractors abruptly decreased to 99,550, and homeworkers decreased to 1,553.

Subcontractors accredited with the GTEB may not, however, be indicative of the total pool, because many subcontracting businesses are in the informal sector and are therefore unregistered. For example, according to the Industry and Trade Statistics Department of the National Statistics Office (NSO), there were 16,067 firms involved in the manufacture of wearing apparel, except footwear, in 1995. Of this number, 12,628 had only 1 to 4 workers, and 1,181, 5 to 9 workers. Usually, microenterprises employing less than ten workers belong to the informal sector.

Policy and Program Implications

What are the policy and program implications of all this? Subcontracted home-workers, through PATAMABA, have explored various tracks in addressing the financial and economic crisis, overcoming its negative effects, and using the crisis as an opportunity for self-empowerment. There are many ways of dealing with current realities, depending on the particular situation of homeworker communities, their level of organization or disorganization as they build up social capital, and the strength of their lobbying, networking, and advocacy to change national and global policies, programs, and trends which affect them negatively.

Obviously, the planning and implementation of truly needs-oriented policies and programs in support of subcontracted women workers' empowerment have to fully consider the latter's productive activities to survive the vicissitudes of the current economic crisis. These activities must also be seen in relation to others; e.g., reproductive activities to maintain home and family and community activities to provide social services, improve environmental conditions, and secure habitat and livelihood. These should be properly valued and equitably shared to relieve the burdens of women and give them opportunities for personal development, better quality employment, and community leadership. The problems and constraints in the conduct of such activities are often intermeshed and cannot be addressed by just one, single, isolated intervention. A holistic, integrated, and comprehensive approach is necessary, a process of many components that can meet both the practical everyday needs and the longer-term strategic interests of women in low-income communities.

Community-Based Organizing as the Key

The process of empowerment involves awareness-raising, confidence- and capability-building, facilitating access to and control over resources, and increasing participation in decision-making in all spheres of life—family, workplace, community, and even the nation at large. A necessary element in this program is organizing women within a community-based context so that together, they can gain the knowledge, the skills, the linkages, and the collective strength to meet their needs and interests. These could pertain to the improvement of their material conditions of existence, (e.g. better working conditions, social protection, skills training, seed capital, technical and marketing assistance, job placement, access to water supply, land and housing security, etc.), or to the strengthening of their positions in terms of power relations vis-à-vis their husbands and other men, including employers, landlords, and government officials.

As women go through each stage of empowerment, they acquire more knowledge, skills, insights, experiences, self-confidence, influence, and negotiating and bargaining strength to produce and reproduce resources at increasing levels through their own initiatives and efforts. They are able to thereby "gain ascendancy in the economic, social, and political arena" (Lazo 1993).

The last point is quite important, given the glass ceiling that prevents poor women from advancing and getting their just share of the fruits of development. Poor women have to expand their horizons beyond their homes and communities to know what is going on in the country and in the world, to link their micro-level realities with the macropicture. Otherwise, they will not be able to advocate for government policies and programs that will really be pro-poor. They will not assert their rights to the resources that will enable them to get out of poverty.

Individual and collective interests need to be balanced so that economic advancement takes place within a group context and in response to community needs. Those who are more empowered because they have more knowledge, resources, and influence should be motivated to exercise leadership and share their strength in order to assist other women who are less empowered. Cooperative ventures could be encouraged as a means by which individual women can advance economically in tandem with the group to which they belong.

It is here that community organizing and building become crucial elements in the empowerment process. Community-based women's organizations, such as the more than 200 chapters PATAMABA has built at the village level, need to be strengthened to ensure the sustainability of their initiatives. Building on such initiatives, community-based efforts of government organizations (GOs), non-governmental organizations (NGOs), funding institutions, and business groups have to be coordinated and anchored on the needs and interests of the people they are working with on the ground.

These initiatives can be directed at shifting to alternative livelihood, addressing gender concerns, ensuring the rights of workers, facilitating access to social security and protection, and linking the micro to the macro through sustained national and international policy and program advocacy.

Shifting to Alternative Livelihood

A survey of 160 respondents in five communities conducted in 1999 clearly showed the financial burden of home-based female subcontracted workers. Piece-rates were stagnant or had been decreasing over time and job orders were declining due to the huge labor supply as well as cutthroat international competition in the product markets, whether catering to the export or home market. Incomes were increasingly insufficient to meet the expenditure needs of the homeworkers' large families.

One important coping mechanism of home-based workers, especially women, was to find other sources of income to compensate for their declining income from subcontracted work. The overwhelming majority of respondents wanted to set up new businesses of their own or become subcontractors themselves, but lacked capital and contacts in the subcontracting chain. The few who did become small subcontractors were not economically well off, although their income was higher than that of the average homeworker. They perceived the biggest obstacle to the dream of having their own businesses to be the lack of capital and funds.

Approximately 30% to 40% of respondents in Malibong Bata, Pandi, 47% of respondents in Taal, Malolos, and 72% of respondents in Balingasa, Quezon City said they had attempted to set up a business. The favorite activities were food and market vending, sari-sari (small neighborhood) stores, and in the case of Malibong Bata, Pandi and Balingasa, Quezon City, sewing and selling clothes and bags. The majority of those who tried setting up a business failed primarily because of insufficient capital, and secondarily due to intense competition from other vendors or stores, and to health reasons.

In places where subcontracting seems to be on the wane and/or brings in woefully inadequate income, the workers suggest a more organized, systematic, and sustainable shift to alternative livelihood. This involves gaining access to breakthrough credit (enough to break out of the poverty cycle—which many micro-credit schemes do not enable), training in business management and cooperatives development, and ensuring stable markets.

In Malibong Bata, Pandi, Bulacan, the women originally thought of concentrating on making products for ready markets, such as patches, T-shirts, kimonos, blouses, etc. But given their lack of access to and control over these markets and the unavailability of sufficient capital to sustain this track, they embarked on a training series for alternative livelihood with the assistance of PATAMABA national trainers and academics and practicum students from the Women and Development Program, College of Social Work and Community Development, University of the Philippines. They tried flower-making, door-mat making, processing vegetable condiments, candle-making, and finally wound up with slipper-making, in which they could apply their sewing and embroidery skills as well as use the machines they already owned or had access to. Starting with a very small loan of P500 (US$10 each) to buy the raw materials, the women were able to produce durable and attractive slippers (some even with customized embroidery), find a ready market for them, make a profit, and repay their small loan after four months. With their reorganized chapter regularly meeting and undergoing leadership and other forms of training, they have now ventured into applying for grants from local government units and filing a P100,000 training cum production proposal with the Regional Office of the Department of Labor and Employment (DOLE).

In San Vicente, Angono, Rizal, the workers originally thought of individual projects such as setting up a store, putting up a welding shop, sewing with the benefit of an edging machine, buying and selling jewelry, and selling cooked food. The latest protracted calamity (flooding) forced them to embark on a group project instead, with a small P15,000 loan—the production of Christmas balls (which they used to do under subcontracting but realized they can do on their own with proper market access) and doormats (which PATAMABA Rizal, in cooperation with the Informal Sector Coalition, has acquired expertise in). Many of the San Vicente embroiderers are shifting to

Christmas ball production, which is more regular and better-paying. They have also undergone other skills training (mushroom-growing, candle-making, and peanut butter production) through PATAMABA in cooperation with the Informal Sector Coalition in Rizal.

In Sto. Angel, Sta. Cruz, Laguna, most of the women are already engaged in alternative livelihood activities such as cooking and selling rice cakes and spring rolls, vending coconut salad, and sewing. They have also undergone training in candle-making, which they put to good use during All Saints' Day.

In Balingasa, Quezon City, PATAMABA already has a center for lace-making equipped with six sewing machines provided through a training cum production funding package worth P150,000 (about US$3,000) from the Department of Labor and Employment—National Capital Region (DOLE NCR). This was awarded after they successfully managed a smaller project worth P50,000 funded by the same agency. At the same time, the Balingasa chapter also embarked on a vegetable food supplement project worth P200,000 (US$4,000) with assistance from APPROTECH.

Successful negotiation of the shift to or combination with alternative livelihood would entail mobilization of community groups and resources as well as effective networking efforts. This is where information gathered about available resources (including capital, both financial and social) in the specific communities already mentioned above acquires utmost relevance.

Social capital has been defined as "an aspect of social organization that involves relations between persons... the norms, values, and traditions that promote cooperation and reciprocity... and the networks and organizations that permit resolution of common problems—contributing to economic growth and better quality of life" (Kidder 1997:10). Providing credit without paying attention to its impact on social capital can lead to unfortunate results. There are too many cases of organizations falling apart because of financial mismanagement and corruption, with leaders and members ill-prepared to handle money and eventually accusing each other of running away with the booty. If not handled well, there can also be accusations of nepotism and favoritism against those in charge of lending and collecting. Furthermore, members who are unable to repay the loans due to a variety of circumstances are ashamed to attend meetings of their organization and no longer participate in organizational activities (Gamatan, in Pineda Ofreneo 1999). Worse, peer groups formed to guarantee that repayment of loans becomes a collective responsibility when an individual defaults can also collapse and generate negative feelings among members if one or two fail or refuse to pay.

Other problems have to do with values being promoted wittingly or unwittingly by microfinance programs. Without conscious promotion of a "culture of savings and reciprocity," the most likely result of micro-credit provision and the resultant microenterprise development is "individual competitiveness and short-term profit seeking" (Kidder 1997:13). The phenomenon of a handful of successful microentrepreneurs becoming exploitative or abusive employers or subcontractors of women of lesser means is certainly not a welcome sight.

Ideally, group and cooperative projects should be encouraged, and such projects should address the felt needs of the community, thereby contributing to a sense of solidarity and mutual help.

With the present globalized setting as a given, what is needed is sustainable and is a decent livelihood for women homeworkers. This can be achieved only if skills and entrepreneurship are developed, and only if rural and urban economies become dynamic as a result of rural, urban, and regional development. The current recession in East Asia and the boom-bust cycles experienced by the Philippines hardly provide this environment. Globalization forces countries to enter cutthroat competition in the international market, but at the same time, it releases forces causing crises and economic difficulties that reduce their competitiveness. This is why livelihood efforts at the micro- level should be linked to broader initiatives to transform macro-level economic realities.

Addressing Gender Concerns

The Asian financial crisis resulted in an increase in the financial, physical, and psychological burden of subcontracted women workers. The economic difficulties brought about by intensifying competition in both labor and product markets have reduced the earning power of subcontracted women workers. They find themselves burdened with the responsibility of cutting down expenses, incurring debts, and undertaking secondary paid-work activities to increase their sources of income. This is aggravated by the current recession and weather disturbances, which have resulted in men being laid off from their jobs and decreases in their income. Deterioration of physical and social infrastructure has further compounded problems, since constant flooding and problems with peace and order intertwine with economic hardship.

Although women homeworkers see positive benefits to subcontracted home-based work, such as earning income while near their children and inside their homes, using the skills traditionally taught to women such as sewing and embroidery, and gaining self-respect and self-confidence because of their earnings, they are also overburdened with subcontracted, domestic, and nurturing activities consistent with the prevailing gender division of labor.

Results of the focus group discussions in the communities reveal that in the sphere of production, there is general division of labor between women and men, with the former associated with home-based work, pig, fowl, and vegetable-raising, food processing and vending, and the latter with agriculture, fishing, driving, carpentry, plumbing, masonry, and other construction work. Women's incomes tend to be more stable and varied even if lesser paid, while men's work is often seasonal and irregular even if better paid. Thus, women say that their productive work is crucial for family survival because their income is either a "big help" or is actually the main source. In terms of reproductive work, women in all communities are unanimous in saying that men only help when they have no work outside the home, and this is seldom. The situation is greatly exacerbated when women have rush orders requiring them to work 12–16 of their waking hours. The problem is especially acute for women with small children who merely squeeze in their productive work during times when their babies or toddlers are asleep. All are unanimous in saying that having their own income through subcontracted work has provided them a sense of entitlement to make purchases for their own needs (as opposed to collective family needs) and improved their bargaining position vis-à-vis their husbands/partners, thereby bringing them closer to the ideal state of joint decision-making and equal power sharing. Nevertheless, they complain about male entitlements to "vices" (alcohol, cigarettes, drinking parties) and some men's tendencies to be jealous and insecure if their wives/partners are too preoccupied with their productive work, are earning more than they are, or are venturing outside the community to sell their wares.

Case studies provide additional insights to gender issues and relations that could not be obtained from the survey and the focus group discussions. On the one hand, there are incidents of domestic violence (see the case of Esperanza) and infidelity on the part of husbands (as in the case of Maria). On the other hand, possibilities of more egalitarian relations are manifested in the case of Gloria, whose second husband does his share of the housework and assists in all her efforts to support her many children. The husband and wife case (Banaag and Helenita) shows the flexibility of the gender division of labor under conditions of hardship and how it can be changed through awareness-raising within a generally progressive community context. In this case, Banaag engages in home-based work (bag-making) in addition to agriculture, tricycle driving, construction, fish vending, etc. This variety of engagements is necessary so that he and his wife can support their seven children during times of crisis. He and Helenita, both involved in progressive people's organizations for years, have acquired the ethic of gender equity and engage in shared housework and joint decision-making. There is one area, however, where their efforts fell short—family planning. Both were reluctant to use available fertility management methods because of perceived negative side effects. Leaving this matter to chance led to their having seven children, many more than they really want.

Workers during the validation workshop conducted in connection with this research had a few suggestions regarding the gender issues raised. They said that communication and dialogue between husbands and wives should be encouraged, and that children should be raised in a non-sexist way, with boys and girls being taught to share in the housework.

Gender issues need to be addressed, however, not only at the level of the family through fairer burden sharing, more equitable distribution of expenditures and sacrifices, and more democratic decision-making between husband and wife, but among all family members. Community-based initiatives should also be launched, in order to advance gender equity and women's empowerment.

Within the community setting, both women and men should undergo gender awareness seminars. This was successfully attempted in Malibong Bata, Pandi, Bulacan, with the assistance of fieldwork students from the Women and Development Program, University of the Philippines College of Social Work and Community Development (WDP/ UPCSWCD). Informal child-minding arrangements may be created among parents with small children who can take turns round-robin style. Or child-care centers may be instituted through community initiatives in partnership with funding from the barangay (the rough equivalent to a village community government) and support from local government units (LGUs). Such centers should render eight-hour services so that parents can be free to work. In regards to violence against women, women's health, and reproductive rights, awareness campaigns may be conducted and counseling and other specialized services may be provided to those in need through networking with women's NGOs and appropriate LGUs.

Ensuring the Rights of Subcontracted Workers

Obviously, a strategy which concentrates on ensuring the rights of subcontracted workers can only be attempted in communities where subcontracting remains a viable activity. In Sto. Angel Central, papier-mâché making seems to have no future, given the waning orders and the extremely low piece-rates. Homeworkers there have actually transferred to other forms of livelihood. In places like Malibong Bata, Pandi, Bulacan, only those producing patches, potholders, and Barong Tagalog remain under subcontracting. In San Vicente, those engaged in smocking still have continuous orders but are receiving less and less income over time. In Taal, bag-making has more flexibility, since producers can choose to supply subcontractors or market their products themselves. In Balingasa, most of the homeworkers know that the ready-to-wear and other products they are making are delivered to factories. They complain of delayed payments because of the post-dated checks issued by those who provide the orders. In these places, advocacy to implement existing laws meant to protect homeworkers needs to be complemented by efforts to ensure continued income from alternative sources in case subcontractors stop giving orders to workers who have the courage to demand their rights.

In the Philippine context, the law on homework has been very much influenced by homeworkers' advocacy. In the early 1990s, PATAMABA, in cooperation with sympathetic government and NGOs, was able to push for the issuance of Department Order No. 5 (DO5) of the Rules Implementing Book III of the Labor Code on Employment of Homeworkers. Among the salient provisions of the rules are the following:

- The right to self-organization of homeworkers and the registration of homeworkers' organizations which "shall be entitled to the rights and privileges granted by law to legitimate labor organizations"

- Registration of employer, contractor, and subcontractor

- Immediate payment for homework after delivery of goods and remittance by the contractor/subcontractor or employer of contributions to the Social Security System (SSS), Medicare, and the Employees Compensation Commission (ECC)

- Standard output rates determined by time and motion studies to equalize piece-rates received by workers in the factory or main undertaking of the employer and homeworkers performing the same job or activity, individual/collective agreement between employers and homeworkers, or tripartite consultations with representatives of government, employers, and workers

- Prohibition of any deduction from homeworkers' earnings for materials lost, destroyed, soiled, or damaged save for certain conditions

- Requirement for homeworker to redo work improperly executed or returned only once without payment

- Liability of the employer, jointly and severally with the contractor or subcontractor if the latter fails to pay the wages or earnings of his/her workers

- Regulation of employment of minors as homeworkers

- Prohibition of homework in dangerous occupations

- Assistance by the Department of Labor and Employment (DOLE) Regional office to registered homeworkers' organizations, employers, contractors, and subcontractors regarding information on wages and other benefits, conduct of time and motion studies to ensure fair and reasonable output rates; skills training; maintenance of safe and healthful conditions at the workplace; information on entitlement to social security and employees compensation benefits; facilitation of loans with government and non-government financial institutions; and information on availment of housing programs under the government-run housing fund (PAG-IBIG)

In San Vicente, Angono, time and motion studies involving embroidery and Christmas ball workers have been conducted by the DOLE in cooperation with PATAMABA as steps toward the implementation of D.O. 5. As earlier mentioned, many of the embroidery workers in the community are shifting to Christmas ball production, especially after they were able to negotiate a higher piece-rate (from six to ten pesos per ball) from the subcontractor using the results of the time and motion study as a basis.

Most homeworkers' groups, however, are nonetheless reluctant to serve as test cases for such implementation. This reluctance is due to the risks and costs encountered when workers assert their rights under the law. There was reference to the case of the sawali (bamboo) weavers of Bataan who tried to hold their subcontractor liable for non-payment of work. They lost their orders while the subcontractor transferred the work to other sawali-weaving communities. Other constraints are the time lost and the expenses occurred in following up cases that have to be filed in faraway Regional Offices of DOLE.

PATAMABA national officials also say that during times of crisis, the interest of workers is to keep whatever livelihood they already have—better to eat rice gruel than to have none at all. If pursuing their rights under the law will only result in having nothing rather than a little something, the choice is quite obvious. What some of the homeworkers suggest is to attempt a test case in a community where those involved already have an alternative livelihood they can rely on just in case they lose their orders. There are also those who say that a non-confrontational approach may work— e.g., engaging in dialogue with subcontractors and principals, or asking friendly sub-contractors to mediate between principals (or employer) and homeworkers. The assumption in this approach is that these subcontractors are allies of the workers on the strength of their kinship or neighborly relations with them. Of particular interest to homeworkers is ensuring a clear contract between themselves and their subcon-tractors and facilitation of their membership in the Social Security System (SSS) to be able to claim sickness, maternity, disability, retirement, and death benefits. They also want to receive the piece-rates due them, to be paid on time, and to have fair com-pensation for rejects that they have redone.

In terms of advocacy plans, PATAMABA was also considering pushing for a Magna Carta for Homeworkers. This is in light of the fact that D.O. 5 covers those under sub-contracting but not the self-employed. Initial dialogues with NGOs and sympathetic legislators, however, have convinced PATAMABA that it may be more fruitful to push for a Magna Carta for Informal Sector Workers to widen the base of support for advo-cacy. Timing may also be off in terms of pushing for any new legislation, given the spate of laws already approved but lacking funding due to government's tight fiscal position. Adding one more law to the list of non-implementable ones may not be worth the gargantuan effort of having a pro-worker bill pass through the legislative mill dom-inated by employers and other vested interests.

The homeworkers are also advocating that the Philippine government immedi-ately ratify ILO Convention 177 (The Homework Convention 1996) and the accompanying Homework Recommendation 1996 which has provisions similar to D.O. 5 but provides more clarity or goes even further in the areas of data collection, the rights to organize and to bargain collectively, remuneration, occupational safety and health, hours of work, rest periods, leave, social security and maternity protec-tion, protection in case of termination of employment, and programs related to home-work. The Recommendation provides the following, among others:

- Detailed information, including data classified according to sex, on the extent and characteristics of homework

- Information in writing or any other manner to the homeworker regarding the name and address of the employer and intermediary, the rate of remuneration and methods of calculation, and the type of work to be performed

- Requirement for employers to keep a register of all homeworkers, classified according to sex, to whom they give work, as well as a record of work given to each homeworker

- Encouragement of collective bargaining as a means of determining the terms and conditions of work of homeworkers

- Compensation to homeworkers for "(a) costs incurred in connection with their work, such as those relating to use of energy and water, communications and maintenance of machinery and equipment; and (b) time spent in maintaining machinery and equipment, changing tools, sorting, unpacking and packing, and other such operations"

- Dissemination of guidelines concerning the safety and health regulations and precautions that employers and homeworkers are to observe

- Daily and weekly rest for homeworkers comparable to that enjoyed by other workers irrespective of deadlines

- The same protection of homeworkers as that provided to other workers with respect to termination of employment

- Programs related to homework, including among others, awareness-raising on homework-related issues among employers' and workers' organizations, NGOs, and the public at large; facilitating organizing homeworkers in organizations of their own choosing, including cooperatives; training carried out as close as practicable to workers' homes and not requiring unnecessary formal qualifications; facilitating homeworkers' access to equipment, tools, raw materials, and other essential materials that are safe and of good quality; facilitating creation of centers and networks for homeworkers to provide them with information and services and reduce their isolation; facilitating access to credit, improved housing and childcare; and promoting recognition of homework as valid work experience

PATAMABA is already part of an Informal Sector Coalition, together with the Trade Union Congress of the Philippines (TUCP), Balikatan sa Kaunlaran (BSK), KALIPI, and others to push for the ratification of ILO Convention 177 and the implementation of D.O. 5. The Coalition had a national congress in April 1999 and is doing work in five pilot areas with funding from the United States Agency for International Development (USAID). It has conducted signature campaigns supporting ILO Convention 177 and has submitted the results to sympathetic senators in Congress.

Homeworkers under PATAMABA are also supportive of another law—Department Order (D.O.) No. 10 Series of 1997—amending the rules implementing Books III and VI of the Labor Code as amended, governing subcontracting in general. Following are the significant provisions of D.O. 10:

- Recognizes principle of business flexibility but not at the expense of labor—"Flexibility for the purpose of increasing efficiency and streamlining operations is essential for every business to grow in an atmosphere of free competition; however, any form of flexibility intended to circumvent or evade workers' rights shall in no case be countenanced" (Sec. 1.C, Rule VIII, Book III)

- Recognizes trilateral relationship among contracting parties—"A contracting or subcontracting arrangement involves a trilateral relationship under which there is a contract for a specific job, service, or work between the principal and the contractor or subcontractor, and a contract of employment between the contractor or subcontractor and its workers" (Sec. 3, Rule VIII-A, Book III)

- Defines legitimate contracting or subcontracting as follows: i) The contractor or subcontractor carries on a distinct and independent business and undertakes to perform the job, work, or service on its own account and under its own responsibility, according to its own manner and method, and free from the control and direction of the principal in all matters connected with the performance of the work except as to the results thereof; ii) The contractor or subcontractor has substantial capital or investment; and iii) The agreement between the principal and contractor or subcontractor assures the contractual employees entitlement to all labor and occupational safety and health standards, free exercises of the right to self-organization, security of tenure, and social and welfare benefits

- Lists permissible types of contracting and subcontracting

- Expressly prohibits among others, labor-only contracting, contracting out of work which will either displace employees of the principal from their jobs or reduce their regular work hours, taking undue advantage of the economic situation or lack of bargaining strength of the contractual employee, undermining their security of tenure or basic rights, or circumventing the provisions of regular employment

- Reiterates that the contractual employee shall be "entitled to all the rights and privileges due to a regular employee

- Specifies that the contract between the contractor or subcontractors and the contractual employees shall include the specific description of the job, work, or service, the place of work, and terms and conditions of employment, including duration and the wage rate

- Stresses the joint and solitary liability of principals when the contractor or sub-contractor is not registered, commits prohibited activities, or is declared guilty of unfair labor practice

- Requires contractors and subcontractors to register with the regional offices or the Bureau of Labor Relations of the Department of Labor and Employment (DOLE)

PATAMABA national officials say that implementation of D.O. 10 is weak, however, as indicated by the paucity of contractors and subcontractors who actually register with the DOLE.

Facilitating Access to Social Security and Protection

Regarding membership in the Social Security System (SSS), Government Service Insurance System (GSIS), or Pag-Ibig (Government Housing Loan Fund), 95% of respondents from Sto. Angel, Sta. Cruz, 85.7% from Taal, Malolos, 84.1% from Malibong Bata, Pandi, 56.3% from San Vicente, Angono, and 40% from Balingasa, Quezon City said they were not members of any security system. Significantly, the more urbanized communities—Balingasa, Quezon City and San Vicente, Angono—had more respondents who were members of the government insurance system. A larger number of respondents in these communities worked in the formal private or government sectors. The common reasons for not being a member of the social security system were lack of knowledge of how to become a member, lack of time to fix the necessary papers and requirements, and inability to fulfill requirements such as providing income tax returns.

The Philippines is a signatory to ILO Convention 102 defining social security as ". . . the protection which society provides its members . . . against the economic and social distress that otherwise would be caused by the stoppage or substantial reduction of earnings resulting from sickness, maternity, employment injury, unemployment, invalidity, old age and death; the provision of medical care; and the provision of subsidies for families with children."

Two state-run institutions provide social security in the form of sickness, maternity, disability, retirement, and death benefits: the Government Service Insurance System (GSIS), which covers government employees; and the Social Security System (SSS), which covers workers in the private sector. The combined membership of these two institutions amounts to 20.67 million in 1997, or only 65.3% of the total labor force. Many vulnerable sectors are not covered and therefore not ensured social protection as mandated by the Philippine Constitution, even if theoretically, they can all apply for membership. Among them are subcontracted, casual, probationary, temporary, and other forms of "flexible" workers; farmers and fisherfolk; migrants; indigenous communities; self-employed and other workers in the informal sector. The social protection provided is also inadequate if measured against the ILO definition, because it does not or scarcely includes unemployment benefits (which are very much needed given the impact of globalization and the economic crisis), and subsidies for families with children (Amante, Serrano, and Ortiz, in Ofreneo and Serrano 1999).

Aside from those offered by the SSS and the GSIS, there are also non-governmental social security arrangements provided by private institutions such as life insurance corporations, health maintenance organizations, NGOs, cooperatives, religious groups, and extended family systems. In many households, especially in the research sites, care of the elderly and of young children is family-based rather than institution-based.

The SSS is under pressure from the Department of Finance (as well as certain unnamed "international bodies") to undergo privatization or to perform at the same level as private fund managers, which is a trend in social security worldwide. SSS officials are resisting this pressure for the moment, considering it the moral obligation of the government to provide social security to the poor who will have to pay higher contributions in case of privatization.

PATAMABA since its inception has lobbied for homeworkers' membership in the SSS. Its leaders have made several presentations to SSS officials to hammer out special arrangements for homeworkers but to no avail. One difficulty for subcontracted homeworkers is the identification of employers who will shoulder part of the SSS contributions. With no such identification, membership is not possible unless entry is placed under the category "self-employed." But to gain membership as self-employed, an individual has to shoulder the entire contribution, which can be quite heavy for small income-earners. Under these circumstances, few PATAMABA members can gain access to state-provided social security. So far, only some self-employed homeworkers in two provinces (Iloilo and Rizal) have succeeded in becoming SSS members, paying a monthly contribution of slightly more than a hundred pesos. Such membership was facilitated by their leaders, who collected individual applications and submitted them in batches to SSS offices.

PATAMABA national leaders and some from the provinces have opted to avail themselves of the services of the Co-op-Life Mutual Benefit Services Association (CLIMBS) for burial benefits. CLIMBS was organized by a federation of cooperatives in Mindanao Island in 1971 to provide mutual protection to subscribing cooperatives and their members. It now has more than 92,000 individual enrollees in 265 member primaries (Gonzalez, in Ofreneo and Serrano 1999).

PATAMABA chapters also have indigenous social protection schemes such as the damayan, whereby members commit themselves to a certain amount of contribution when a fellow-member dies or gets sick. The contributions usually cover funeral expenses and food served during the wake. Aside from monetary aid, damayan members also cook and serve during the wake and attend the burial in full force.

Given these realities, PATAMABA leaders suggest that subcontracted homeworkers who are also self-employed be registered under the latter category in the SSS if they are in a hurry and can afford the monthly contribution. Those who are ready to assert their rights as subcontracted workers can advance in the direction of identifying their employer and making the latter remit contributions to the SSS. In either case, PATAMABA leaders would be there to assist these workers. Non-governmental and indigenous schemes can also be promoted on a community basis among those who are interested.

LINKING THE MICRO AND THE MACRO

Analysis and intervention, as the homeworkers themselves pointed out during the validation workshop for the research, should encompass the various spheres of women's lives, from the micro to the macro.

Changes should occur in marriage and family relations in order to promote shared parenting and housework, equitable division of labor, and democratic decision-making, as well as to address and prevent violence and abuse directed at women and children. Expensive male entitlements to cigarettes, alcohol, and leisure activities (such as drinking and partying with friends) during times of crisis should give way to a fairer distribution of expenditures and sacrifices between husband and wife and among family members in general. Domestic violence, infidelity, neglect of women's reproductive rights, and the continuing practice of child labor have to be addressed at the micro-level.

At the level of the community, gender, livelihood, and environmental issues have to be problematized and solved collectively. This is where the notion of social capital becomes important. The more experience women's, people's, and NGOs have in discussing and addressing community problems together in a spirit of solidarity and mutual support, the stronger the chances of success will be.

Childcare and women's health issues, for example, can be addressed through community effort. Women with small children can come together and create informal child-minding services for themselves in round-robin fashion, instead of relying on older women (grandmothers, grand-aunts, and other kin who also have work to do) to look after toddlers and preschoolers to enable them to concentrate on their livelihood activities. Community-based women's groups can advocate for better health services and spearhead campaigns on reproductive rights and on violence against women and children.

Campaigns to improve working conditions under subcontracting and efforts to engage in dialogues and negotiations with subcontractors, contractors, and employers can be facilitated through community-based mechanisms and kinship relations.

Access to credit, training, and technical and marketing assistance for alternative livelihood can be facilitated through networking among GOs, NGOs, POs, women's groups, and funding institutions (e.g., cooperatives, rural banks, etc.) found within or rendering services within the community. As emphasized earlier, credit should be substantial enough to enable the recipients to break out of the poverty cycle, and not remain on a poverty-level treadmill. This need for increasing aggregate amounts for re-lending can be met by extensive networking with government agencies, local government units, and international aid agencies. This is what the Balingasa chapter of PATAMABA has been doing, and its example is being followed by other homeworker communities in Malibong Bata and San Vicente. But microfinancing programs and microenterprises that go with them can make a real and lasting difference in poor women's lives only if they are integrated into a more comprehensive program of empowerment. In other words, they should work in tandem with other development interventions. Increased income is not the only need women have. They also need control over their fertility, protection from male violence, access to other resources such as land, water, housing, etc., as well as education and training to raise their awareness, develop their capabilities, and fulfill their human potential in solidarity with other women and with other members of the community. Microenterprise development can never be a substitute for asset or structural reforms (such as land and aquatic reform) and social services such as health care, family planning, childcare, environmental sanitation, and protection.

Environmental problems such as intermittent flooding, lack of garbage disposal facilities, pollution, etc., can be addressed by sustained community advocacy and initiatives. Issues concerning degradation of agricultural land (e.g., the negative effect of land conversion for golf courses, etc.) and fishing grounds (e.g., pollution and fishpond proliferation in Laguna Lake) require more concerted action by farmer and fisher groups strengthened by solid community support. In regards to land, environmental, and other community issues raised, workers suggest awareness campaigns as well as concrete community initiatives such as zero waste management, clean and green projects, etc. They propose more effective networking with GOs and NGOs concerned with drug addiction, pollution, foot-and-mouth disease, etc.

Micro-level interventions should be linked to macro-level realities that need to be transformed, such as the removal of the "glass ceiling" which prevents women and the poor in general from advancement. Only women who are aware and organized can engage in advocacy towards more gender-responsive and pro-poor policies and programs. For example, in the face of the contraction of credit due to the effects of the financial and economic crisis, IMF austerity measures, and the demands of structural adjustments, women's groups can lobby together for more financial resources in the form of new safety nets for those severely affected by the crisis, or for more substantial allocations from funds earmarked for poverty alleviation. Capacity building for microfinance institutions is supposed to be provided by the People's Development Trust Fund (PDTF) created by the Poverty Alleviation Act (Llanto and Lirio 1998:17). Women's groups can attempt to gain access to such a Fund as a form of affirmative action.

Given the emphasis on food security, which is a women's domain in the realm of household economics, more money should be released for not only basic grains, which are farmed predominantly by men, but also for vegetable raising, small livestock production, food processing, distribution, and storage facilities managed by women. The debates on the future of agrarian reform in the country can lend space to accommodate women's continuing demand for land rights, because access to land is the key to women's economic empowerment in rural areas.

Advocacy can be taken one step further, as in the case of the women in El Salvador who are lobbying for a National Credit Policy that will result in an autonomous institution to be run by financial experts, government officials, and representatives of women's NGOs for the provision of credit and guarantee funds for women's microenterprises, small enterprises, and medium enterprises (Kidder 1997:15). In the Philippine case, the National Credit Council Policy Guidelines for Credit Programs as well as the National Strategy for Microfinance have no specific provisions addressing women's needs and interests (Llanto and Lirio 1998). Women's groups could advocate for the inclusion of such provisions.

In the Philippine case, women's groups can also participate in efforts such as the Jubilee 2000 which seeks freedom from onerous debt, and repeal of the automatic appropriation for debt service provision which enables the Chief Executive to set aside huge amounts of the budget for repayment of loans, thereby decreasing the funds left for economic and social development.

All the efforts at the micro-level should be linked together in order to exert influence at the national, regional, and global levels, especially given the largely negative impact of globalization and the financial and economic crisis. The conditions of homeworkers are invariably shaped by the changing nature of the global economy as manifested in national and regional macroeconomic trends. As explained during the validation workshop, globalization, specifically trade liberalization, has resulted in more exports for the Philippines and other states, and more and cheaper imports from other countries. The result is increased competition within the Philippines among producers of the same goods, as well as from other countries, as in the case of Philippine-made garments, bags, and shoes which are losing in the domestic market because of the influx of cheap imports. Philippine-based exporters are losing in the global market because prices of exports from China, India, Bangladesh, Indonesia, Thailand, etc., are cheaper due to the much lower wages received by workers in these countries. The situation is aggravated by bad infrastructure facilities and the high cost of power and other utilities in the Philippines. As a result of all these factors, homeworkers under subcontracting suffer from lower income, reduced expenditures, and greater indebtedness. They have to search for additional or alternative livelihood but are hamstrung by lack of capital and markets.

Given the above linkages, homeworkers can explore several points of advocacy. They can call for reasonable import controls, such as preventing the reduction of tariffs beyond what is necessary to honor international obligations, and for government support in terms of loans and technical and marketing assistance. However, the constraints here include the government's tight fiscal position in relation to IMF-imposed austerity measures, and its continuing inability to provide for "safety nets" for sectors adversely affected by globalization and the economic crisis. The government is also committed to the neoliberal model of development and is advocating an even greater opening up of the economy as evidenced by the proposed constitutional changes allowing foreigners to own land. This kind of development model has not worked for the Philippines in the past 35 years or so, however, when the country came under IMF and World Bank tutelage and structural adjustment programs. The only long-term solution to homeworkers' problems is to improve the general politico-economic situation towards providing more and quality jobs for all in need. The outlook for this is not bright, considering the government's current economic thrusts and political propensities which including "kowtowing" to foreign interests, bringing back the Marcos cronies, and threatening press and other freedoms. Even so, pressure needs to be brought to bear on the state to provide facilities for credit, markets, skills development, and capacity building for homeworkers and other vulnerable groups reeling from globalization.

The negative politico-economic environment also limits possibilities for legal advocacy, given the generally weak bargaining position of workers and their fear of losing whatever jobs they already have if they assert their rights without the necessary support. Still, there is space for awareness-raising regarding laws that are meant to protect homeworkers and workers under subcontracting in general at the national, regional, and global levels so that those who are prepared to claim their legal rights can do so because they are already there. Access to more assistance for groups that are vulnerable to the negative impact of globalization and the economic crisis should also be advocated for in United Nations bodies, multilateral institutions, international development agencies, and funding sources.

In the global arena, labor rights advocates claim that the increasingly negative assessment of the impact of unbridled globalization on workers, women, and other vulnerable groups creates a space for asserting international regulations such as the social clause in the WTO, implementing corporate codes of conduct covering employment conditions, commitment to equal opportunities, prohibition of child labor and forced labor, and environmental protection initiated by multinational corporations such as Levi Strauss, Liz Claiborne, Reebok, Nike, The Gap, and Starbucks (Tan and Reeves 1996:35). However, they also maintain that workers, including the unemployed, the informal sector, and migrants, should be the primary actors in this endeavor and that the trade union movement should reinvent itself by being more inclusive and by developing new forms of representation and organization (Challenging Globalisation 1999:29).

Women Working Worldwide (WWW), which conducted consultations with workers' groups in Bangladesh, India, Indonesia, Pakistan, the Philippines, and Sri Lanka, says that "as long as workers remain marginalised from the development, implementation, and monitoring of codes, then the value of these codes will be questionable." Workers consulted assert that these codes, which cover only a few workers producing for export, should not be a substitute for stronger national legislation and implementation of existing laws protecting workers' rights. These codes could supplement national legislation, however, and could be useful if monitored by independent agencies. The workers suggest that these codes cover trade union rights, which for the most part are not currently included (Clean Clothes 1999).

Given this context, homeworkers in the Philippines can add their voice to increasing advocacy efforts by international labor movements seeking to reassert workers' rights in the global arena in the face of their increasing erosion, due to the negative impact of globalization. This is in the light of the fact that the Philippines is quite advanced in terms of labor legislation and has ratified all major ILO Conventions (save for No. 177 on homework) covering fundamental workers' rights (freedom of association—Nos. 87, 98, and 141), abolition of forced labor (105), equality of opportunity and treatment (100, 111, 138), employment (88, 122, 159), labor administration (144), conditions of work (94, 95, 99), social security (118, 157, 17, 19), night work for women (89), and employment of children and young persons (59, 77, 90). The point is to realize the spirit of all these conventions in the everyday life of all working people, especially those made even more vulnerable by globalization.

REFERENCES

Amante, M.S.V., M.R. Serrano, and I.A. Ortiz. 1999. Social Security and Labor Insecurities Under Globalization. In *Social Security and Labor Insecurities Under Globalization*, edited by Rene E. Ofreneo and Melisa R. Seranno. Diliman, Quezon City: School of Labor and Industrial Relations, University of the Philippines.

Challenging Globalisation: Solidarity and Search for Alternatives. 1999. *Proceedings of an Asia-Europe Joint Consultation* organized by the Asian Migrant Center (AMC), Asia Monitor Resource Center (AMRC), Asia Alliance of YMCAs (AAYMCA), Asian Human Rights Commission (AHRC), Asian Regional Exchange for New Alternatives (ARENA), Committee for Asian Women (CAW) and Documentation for Action Groups in Asia (DAGA). Hong Kong, October.

Gonzalez, E.T. 1999. Non-Governmental Social Security Arrangements. In *Social Security and Labor Insecurities under Globalization*, edited by Ofreneo and Serrano. Diliman, Quezon City: School of Labor and Industrial Relations, University of the Philippines.

Involving Workers in the Debate on Company Codes: Women Working Worldwide's Education and Consultation Project. 1990. In *Clean Clothes newsletter*, No. 11. August, Amsterdam.

Lazo, L.S. 1993. Some Reflections on the Empowerment of Homeworkers. In *From the Shadows to the Fore–Practical Actions for the Social Protection of Homeworkers in the Philippines*. Bangkok: International Labour Organization Regional Office for Asia and the Pacific.

Lim, J.Y. 1999. The Effects of Globalization and the East Asian Crisis on Employment of Women and Men: The Philippine Case. In *World Development*, 28 (7), Washington D.C.

Llanto, G. and R.P. Lirio. 1998. Toward a Microfinance Policy and Regulatory Framework: The Philippines. In *Microfinancing Regional Dialogue*, ACFOD, ACCU, and CDF, June 1–3, Bangkok.

Ofreneo, P. 1999. Towards Women's Empowerment: Integrating Gender Concerns in Micro Finance. Paper prepared for the National Workshop Conference on Promoting Gender-Responsive Microfinancing Programs, June 28–30, Estaca Beach Resort, Compostela, Cebu.

Ofreneo, R.E. and M.R. Serrano, eds. 1999. *Social Security and Labor Insecurities under Globalization*. Diliman, Quezon City: School of Labor and Industrial Relations, University of the Philippines.

Sharpston, M. 1975. International Subcontracting. In *Oxford Economic Papers*. Oxford, March.

Tan, L.L. and D. Reeves. 1996. *Labor Standards in a Global Economy—Issues and Options*. Maryland: Bread for the World Institute.

Women Homeworkers and the Asian Crisis. 1999. Homeworkers' Network/ *HOMENET Southeast Asia*. Manila: SEAGAP Singapore.

Note: This chapter is based on research conducted in five communities of subcontracted women workers in 1998 for the Asia Foundation. The study involved a variety of research methods: a survey of 160 worker-respondents (mostly women and including a few men, PATAMABA members and non-members); community profiles; focus group discussions; and case studies.

6

Subcontracted Women Workers in the Garment Industry in India

Jeemol Unni and Namrata Bali

The garment industry, especially the export sector of the industry, is one in which women account for about one-fourth of the total employment. This industry is also poised for rapid growth in the post-liberalization and post-General Agreement on Trade and Tariffs (GATT) years. According to the Lalbhai group, a prominent textile and garment manufacturing industrial house in India, "A typical garment-manufacturing unit is very small. Manufacturing units having fifty machines are about 6% of the total manufacturing units. A majority of the units work as subcontractors and are known as fabricators in the industry parlance. These fabricators account for about 77% of the sewing machine capacity. Manufacturer exporters account for only 7.5% of the machine capacity. The size of the units do not allow these units to innovate, to upgrade their products and operations and to build brands," (Lalbhai et al. undated). Most of the units consequently compete at the lower end of the market. Thus, the Indian garment sector is based on a subcontracting system where a large number of very small units operate.

The purpose of this chapter is to analyze how the changes in the garment industry affect the situation of women working in subcontracting arrangements. This is placed in the overall context of the garment industry in India. This research is based on secondary data as well as primary data collected in a city in India, Ahmedabad. In the second section of the chapter the structure and size of the garment industry in India is presented. In section three the national and international policies that affect the garment industry in India is reviewed. In the fourth section the garment industry in Ahmedabad is analyzed and three cases of subcontracting chains within the garment industry in the city are described to examine how they operate and what the value addition is in the various segments in the chain. In the fifth section how subcontracting affects women workers in this industry and its impact on their double-role in the household is analyzed.

STRUCTURE OF THE GARMENT INDUSTRY

The garment industry had its origins in India during the Second World War, when such units were set up for mass production of military uniforms. The industry grew fast, mainly due to the shift in urban consumer tastes from custom-tailored garments to ready-made garments and the introduction of export promotion schemes by the Government. According to a comprehensive survey conducted by the Textile Committee (Ministry of Textiles 1991), the industry consists of four types of units, namely domestic manufacturers, manufacturer-exporters, fabricators, and merchant-exporters/traders. It is the process of production which allows for decentralized production and scope for subcontracting. The industry consists of small and cottage units, with less than 11 workers, which accounts for 80% of the units; and medium (with 21–49 workers) and large (more than 49 workers) units accounting for 14 and 6% respectively. The industry is of relatively recent origin, with about 42% of the units set up during 1986–89, and 30% during 1981–85 (Batra 1996). Of course, a large number of units may have been set up post-1990.

There are two important sources of data on the manufacturing industry in India. The large units registered under the Indian Factories Act, 1948 are covered by the Annual Survey of Industries. This consists of units with more than 10 workers with power and more than 20 workers without power. The smaller units not registered with the Factories Act are surveyed every five years by the National Sample Survey Organization in the Survey of Unorganized Manufacturing Sector. In 1994–95, according to the Annual Survey of Industries, 228,899 workers were engaged in the manufacture of garments and clothing accessories and generated a net value added of Rs.22,903 million. In the unorganized sector, in 1994–95 there were 411,637 workers engaged in the manufacture of garment and clothing accessories generating a gross value added of Rs.7,844 million. Obviously the large units generated a much higher value added per worker, probably accounting for the upper end of the fashion garments. The smaller units in the unorganized sector, however, formed the bulk of the garment industry in terms of the number of units and workers. We present the growth of this sector during the period 1978–79 to 1994–95.

At the all-India level, the garment industry in the unorganized sector seems to have grown the most during the period 1978–85. In fact, the period just before the economic reforms, 1985–90, saw a large decline in the growth of units, workers, and value added. The period since the reforms appears favorable to the garment industry with a positive growth of 1.4% in workers, 3.1% in value added, and 1.8% in labor productivity. The garment industry in Gujarat did not appear to grow much prior to the economic reforms. However, since 1990 the number of units and workers in the industry grew at more than 10% per annum.

Growth of Subcontracted Work in Manufacturing in India

Production in the manufacturing sector in India is increasingly based on subcontracting arrangements between firms. Evidence on this is, however, difficult to obtain. Some indirect and direct evidence available from the existing literature is presented here.

Indirect Evidence

There was a secular decline in the absolute number of workers in the household manufacturing sector over the Population Censuses of 1961, 1981, and 1991, from 50% of the total manufacturing workforce to less than half. This was accompanied by a corresponding increase in the proportion of workforce in the non-household segment. There was a decline in the factory sector's share in total manufacturing employment, from 26% in 1972–73 to 20% in 1993–94. From these two trends it is deduced that there must be an increase in the non-factory, non-household segment of the manufacturing sector (Nagraj 1999). This is likely to be the segment where subcontracting units flourish.

Further evidence is provided of growth in the factories of employment size 0–49 and 50–499, i.e., the small- and medium-sized units compared to the large-sized ones. The small-scale sector, defined in terms of investment of up to Rs.1 million, witnessed the highest growth within the manufacturing sector (Ramaswamy 1999). It is inferred from this evidence of the growth of the small- and medium-sized factories that subcontracting has grown in the period (Nagraj 1999).

Direct Evidence

In a recent survey, conducted in 1996–97, of about 2,000 small-scale units spread over 61 districts in 12 states of India, a direct question was canvassed on whether the unit undertook subcontract work. About 40% of the firms reported that they undertook some form of subcontracted work. The extent of subcontracting was measured as a percent of the sales or activity. It was observed that nearly 25% of the units undertook the activity up to 30% of their turnover (Morris, et al. 1999).

Using the same data set, another study estimated the extent of subcontracting in the small-scale units surveyed by industry groups. The inter-firm linkages, especially the subcontracting type, depend mainly upon the product characteristics such as technologically separable production processes and the possibility of viable production stages. The nature of the production process of metal products and transport equipment allows for subcontracting. These are also included in the reserved list of products for SSIs.

These factors together account for the fact that more than 50% of the units surveyed were engaged in subcontracting in the product groups of basic metals and alloys, metal products and parts, machinery, and equipment other than transport and transport equipment and parts (Pani 1999). Other industry groups with a substantial proportion of units engaged in subcontracting were paper and paper products, leather and leather products, rubber, plastic, petroleum and coal products, wood products, and textile products. Subcontracting units in the cotton textile industry was high, but the sample size was relatively small.

A study utilizing the most widely used official data on the organized (formal) manufacturing sector, the Annual Survey of Industries, has tried to estimate the extent of subcontracting in India (Ramaswamy 1999). Labor contracting and the putting out system are two of the most common forms of subcontracting practices.

The use of contract labor was the highest in two industry groups: beverages and tobacco and the non-metallic mineral products. Bidi-making, within the first industry group, is mainly conducted through this system of contract labor. The other industry groups with a high share of contract labor are food products, basic metals, wool and silks, and chemical products.

A traditional form of the putting out system is when industrial firms supply raw materials to other factories for treatment, finishing, and processing. Data on the value of work done by other concerns (factories and workshops) on material supplied is a measure of the value of subcontracting activity. For large factories, the value of such activity constituted about 5.3% of value added in 1973–74 and 4.5% in 1993–94. For the registered manufacturing sector it was estimated at 8% in 1983–84 and 7% in 1993–94. For large factories it was estimated to be 56% of value added in textile garments and the value of such activity exceeded the reported net value added in the industry group manufacture of fabricated metal products. This type of subcontracting activity was insignificant in all of the other industry groups (Ramaswamy 1999).

Ramaswamy (1999) uses a third measure of subcontracting: the value of goods sold in the same condition in which they were purchased and their share in value added as an index of subcontracting intensity. This measures the degree of product subcontracting. The intensity of subcontracting was only about 9.5% in 1970 and rose to 21% in 1978 among large factories. The user group classification showed that the subcontracting intensity was the highest in consumer non-durable, 33%. The average labor intensity was also the highest in this group as well as their share in value added, next only to the basic industries. Subcontracting intensity was also quite high in consumer durable, 20%, followed closely by capital goods, 19%. Basic goods (16%) and intermediate goods (about 10%) had a lower intensity of product subcontracting.

In the large factory sector, among the consumer non-durables, product subcontracting intensity was high in the stationery articles, vegetable oils and fats, canning of foods, coffee, cosmetics, drugs and medicines, and textile garments. Among the consumer durables it was high in refrigeration, metal furniture and fixtures, electric lamps, and motor vehicles and parts. The consumer non-durables have higher subcontracting intensity, probably because of the batch production method. In the group of basic and intermediate goods, process technology and a continuous flow method of production are used, which are less amenable to product subcontracting (Ramaswamy 1999).

Limited Growth of Subcontracting in India

Two factors highlighted above make the conditions for the growth of subcontracting in India conducive. These are segmentation in the labor market with a large component of informal workers, and the large variation in the size structure of the manufacturing industry. The small firms act as a window to access the unorganized labor market. However, evidence available shows that subcontracting has not developed as much as it should have in comparison to Japan or Taiwan (Morris, et al. 1999).

One of the principal reasons is the much slower growth of the manufacturing industry in India. It was constrained by the "Hindu" rate of growth of 3.5% for nearly fifteen years (Morris, et al. 1999). Thus, in areas with a relatively high growth, e.g., around major cities as Delhi, Pane, and Bangalore, subcontracting has begun in a major way (Nagraj 1986). In regions of slow growth such as in and around Calcutta, instead of subcontracting it was merchant capital that mediated relations between small (tiny) and large firms (Banerjee 1981). The increased growth of manufacturing sector in the eighties was conducive to the growth of subcontracting in the West and South and to a limited extent in the North of India. Vendor development emerged as a strategic option in these areas in some of the more dynamic industries, such as engineering firms (Morris, et al. 1999).

Besides growth, other factors include imperfections in the credit market, which create severe biases against lending to small firms. This erodes their bargaining position vis-à-vis large firms. Another important factor that has limited the growth of subcontracting is the lack of exchanges for booking subcontracting capacities (Morris, et al. 1999). However, with liberalization, it can be hoped that some of these constraints to the growth of the small-scale sector and subcontracting will be removed. Similarly, there is a move to set up a "subcontracting exchange" which will facilitate the growth of subcontracting.

A third reason could be that the forms of subcontracting relationships which are developing are perhaps even less visible than firm-to-firm subcontracting and are not captured by any data collection effort. Data collection on subcontracting between firms are also not sought to be captured systematically, as we observed from the earlier section on empirical evidences. Evidence provided refers mainly to the large factory segment and to some extent the small-scale industry. One of the new forms of subcontracting not captured in these data, is the large component of "homeworkers" engaged in manufacturing activity in their homes. In a survey in Ahmedabad city we observed that 24% of the women workers were engaged as "homeworkers" in various manufacturing activities (Unni 2000).

Regulatory Regimes Governing the Garment Industry

There has been a remarkable growth of exports in India's garment sector beginning in the late 1980s. It has grown from U.S. $1,598 million in 1989–90 to $3,675 million in 1995–96. That is, it has more than doubled in the last five years. It constitutes 12% of India's merchandise exports and nearly 16% of its manufactured export. India's share in the world exports of clothing rose from 1.5% in 1980 to 2.6% in 1994. The two major markets for garment exports of developing countries are the United States and the European Economic Community (EEC).

Multi-Fibre Arrangements

The Multi-Fibre Arrangement (MFA) framework for conducting trade in textiles and clothing is a significant departure from the General Agreement on Trade and Tariffs (GATT). GATT's provisions of trade barriers in the form of tariffs are non-discriminatory as they apply to imports from all countries in an equitable manner. The MFA is based on quantitative restrictions or quotas that restrict the import of specific products from specific countries. The developed countries negotiate bilateral agreements with individual trading partners that limit the amount of exports of the latter. India has bilateral trading arrangements with the United States, Canada, EEC, Austria, Sweden, Norway, and Finland under the MFA. There are no international rules governing the international allocation of quotas under MFA. The MFA is targeted only at imports from the developing countries. The restrictions are imposed through geopolitical consideration, which has facilitated the emergence of China as a major force in the textile and clothing market (Chaterjee and Mohan 1993).

The MFA IV came into force in 1991, when the developing countries were hoping it would not be renewed. The Uruguay Round has on its agenda the phasing out of the MFA by 2005. In MFA IV, for the first time there was a recognition that the final objective is the application of GATT rules to trade in textiles. The MFA is to be phased out in four phases: Phase I starting on January 1, 1995, Phase II on January 1, 1998, Phase III on January 1, 2002, and Phase IV on January 1, 2005, when all restrictions will be eliminated. India's garment sector has to gear up to this reality: when there will cease to be any prescribed quota for any country and all countries will have to compete on the basis of factors determined by the market (Chaterjee and Mohan 1993).

The United States has published a list of products that it intends to integrate in each of the stages. The most import intensive products, like shirts and women's outerwear, in which India has an advantage, will not have their quotas removed until 2005. Besides, the permitted quotas will be more generous for the developing countries like India with a permitted growth of 6–7%. Imports for the dominant suppliers like Hong Kong, China, and South Korea have restricted quota growth rates of 0–2% (Ramaswamy and Gray 1999). Thus, the impact of the removal of MFA will be felt severely by India in 2005. In addition, the textile and clothing sector will have tariff rates higher than that for all goods in the post-Uruguay Round. In fact, U.S. tariff rates for apparels were higher relative to all other MFA products even in 2004.

Government Policy and the Garment Industry

The Indian garment export sector is based on a subcontracting system involving a number of small tailoring and fabricating units that operate under contract from a parent firm. Owing to the seasonal nature of demand for Indian garments, this has proven to be a very cost-effective mode of production. But if India wishes to emulate the path of the world's leading garment exporters, it is imperative to create further capacity to process bulk orders, while at the same time retaining the advantage of being able to handle small orders with large variations. Policies will have to be geared towards introducing large assembly lines of production equipped with good quality machinery (Chaterjee and Mohan 1993).

Policy for Small Scale Enterprises

Development of small-scale industries (SSI) has been an important objective of the planning process in India. Reservation of items exclusively for this sector was one of the main planks of the policy. Different kinds of fiscal concession, in the form of lower excise duties, differential taxation, subsidies, and sales rebates are other important sets of protective measures for the SSIs. Various financial and other institutions have also been set up to facilitate the growth of this sector.

The structure of the garment industry is a direct result of the Government of India's policy, the international regulatory regimes, and the nature of the market. The Government of India has reserved the garment industry for the small-scale sector. Investment in the small-scale sector cannot exceed Rs.6 million, or Rs.7.5 million in the case of ancillary units. These limits change from time to time.

Under the existing policy framework, garment units can be allowed investment in plant and machinery beyond the limits prescribed for SSI units only if they undertake an export obligation of 75% of their total production. This export obligation would operate in perpetuity, without any time frame. The export obligation of 75% of their production is limited to a specified period of 10 years even for 100% export-oriented units, which benefit from duty free imports of capital goods and raw materials. An export obligation of 75% in perpetuity has acted as a strong deterrent for large Indian companies to invest in the garment sector (Chaterjee and Mohan 1993).

During the course of our study most of the large industrialists and spokespersons for this sector argued that the SSI status of this industry should be removed. Presently, due to the reservation for the SSI sector, the existing organized Textile Mill Sector cannot expand their activities to manufacture of garments in a big way, as a downstream project of their textile unit. De-reservation is under consideration by the Government of India. However, the implications of this for the large number of small factory units catering to the local markets will have to be carefully reviewed.

Export of Garments

India's garment industry has flourished on account of cotton-based apparel. However, 60% of the international garment trade is accounted for by man-made blended fabrics. India's garment trade has focused on fashion clothing, but in the long run it would be useful to trade in standard garments that are usually based on synthetic or blended fabrics. India has substantial capacity in the manufacture of polyester yarn and fiber, but the duty structure governing the intermediate inputs in the manufacture of these products has made it impossible to supply fabrics to exporters at rates that would enable them to compete effectively in the international market (Chaterjee and Mohan 1993).

The current high cost of synthetic and blended fiber has necessitated the availability of duty exemption schemes. Under the Duty Exemption Scheme, the Government has recently introduced a value-based scheme to enable exporters to import inputs within the overall value of licenses without any quantitative restrictions. This scheme will operate along with the existing quantity-based advance licensing scheme. The new Export Import (Exim) Policy, which came into operation in March 1992, specified standard input-output norms for 1,514 export products covered by the quantity-based advance licensing scheme. Under the new value-based scheme, value addition norms for value based licenses in respect of 1,195 such export products were identified. However, the garment export sector has not benefited from this new dispensation (Chaterjee and Mohan 1993).

Further, no increase in meterage for import of fabrics has been allowed. Under the present Duty Exemption Scheme the value addition requirement has been increased from 33 to 50%. Moreover, all fabrics have been put in the list of sensitive items in respect of which licenses shall be issued with quantity restrictions under value-based licenses (Chaterjee and Mohan 1993). These policies will be detrimental to the growth of garment exports in man-made and blended fibers, which are necessary if, in the long run, markets have to be maintained.

The Exim Policy has facilitated the import of machinery, including second-hand machinery, with export obligations at concessional rates of duty in various industry groups. A concessional import duty of 15% would be levied on import of capital goods if the company gives an export commitment of four times the value of import to be achieved within five years. A concessional import duty of 25% would be applicable on export commitments three times the value of imports to be achieved within four years. However, all these concessions will not be of any use to the garment sector as long as the reservation for the SSI sector remains. This is because availing of any of these benefits would mean going out of the ambit of the small-scale sector (Chaterjee and Mohan 1993).

The quota-controlled regimes, described earlier, have determined the principal export markets for Indian garment exports. The major share of exports have been with the Western Europe countries and North and South America, principally the United States (Table 6.1), growing from 37% in 1985 to 51% in 1991. The export market in the United States declined from 38 to 30% during the same period. The Eastern Europe markets also contracted for Indian exports. There was a small increase in the share of exports to Africa in the 1980s.

A significant feature of the Indian garment trade is the predominance of cotton as the fiber base and the high share of a few items in the composition of the trade. Women's outerwear had a share of 40% in 1991, which reduced marginally to 38% in 1994. Men's shirts made of cotton increased in share from 16 to nearly 18% during the same period.

The United States absorbed nearly 36% of India's total apparel exports in 1993. This was in spite of the quota restrictions on trade. Again, among the items exported to the United States, women's outerwear constituted about 54% of the total. A striking feature of the United States import of garments was that no single country dominated across all product categories.

Table 6.1   Destinations of Indian Garment Exports (1983 to 1991) Values in Rs. Crore and Percentage Shares of Different Markets

Destinations	1985		1987		1989		1991	
	Value	Share	Value	Share	Value	Share	Value	Share
Western Europe	398	37.3	918	49.5	1473	47.7	2733	51.0
North & South America	406	38.0	660	35.6	1030	33.3	1597	29.8
United States	346	32.4	604	32.6	911	29.5	1328	24.8
East Asia	42	3.9	40	2.2	106	3.4	209	3.9
Japan	40	3.7	37	2.0	95	3.1	187	3.5
Eastern Europe	187	17.5	178	9.6	306	9.9	381	7.1
Soviet Union	173	16.2	166	9.0	280	9.1	287	5.4
Oceanic Countries	19	1.8	25	1.4	54	1.7	63	1.2
Western Asia & Northern Africa	10	0.9	18	0.9	89	0.9	301	5.6
Africa	2	0.2	6	0.3	16	0.5	39	0.7
Southeastern Asia	3	0.3	9	0.5	16	0.5	30	0.6
Southern Asia	0	0.0	0.0	0.1	0	0.0	0	0.0
Northwestern Europe	0	0.0	0.0	0.0	0	0.0	0.0	0.0
Grand Total	1068	100.0	1857	100.0	3091	100.0	5358	100.0

Source: Handbook of Export Statistics, Various issues, Apparel Export Promotion Council. (Quoted in Chaterjee and Mohan 1993).

GARMENT INDUSTRY IN AHMEDABAD

Industrial Growth in Ahmedabad

Ahmedabad is a metropolitan city located in the highly industrialized and urbanized state of Gujarat. The city economy of Ahmedabad began an upswing in 1861, when the first modern textile mill was located in the city. Since then, the growth of textile mills continued and also led to migration of labor, mostly the working class, into the city. The global recession of the 1930s and the communal riots of the 1940s, slowed down the growth in the city, as it saw the closure of a number of textile mills. However, the textile mills revived after the recession and continued to flourish.

The economic structure of the city witnessed considerable change since the 1960s, with the diversification of industrial activity into a number of chemical, petrochemical and other engineering industries in the eastern and western peripheries. However, the dominant and dynamic textile industry more or less stagnated during this period, with no growth in employment. Employment in the city of Ahmedabad grew at the rate of 2.8% over the three decades of 1961–91, according to the Population Census. The fastest growing sector was the construction sector, followed by trade and commerce and transport, storage and communications. The overall growth, however, hides the changes in employment that have been occurring across the industrial sectors in the city over the three decades.

Employment in the manufacturing sector in Ahmedabad grew by about 2.3% per annum from 1961 to 1971. The 1970s saw a slight increase in the growth rate of employment, to 3.2%. However, there was a sharp decline of manufacturing sector growth to 0.4% per annum in the 1981–91 decade. The seriousness of the situation in the urban economy of Ahmedabad is evident from this fact of almost stagnant employment in the manufacturing sector. The growth rate in employment in the construction industry rose tremendously during the 1981-91 period in the city. This could have been the result of urbanization and industrialization, where construction work absorbs a large proportion of labor. The growth rate was also observed to consistently increase in other services over the three decades.

While the organized manufacturing sector in the state of Gujarat, units registered under the Indian Factories Act, was growing consistently during 1978 to 1995, the organized sector in Ahmedabad city was expected to have suffered a major setback due to the closure of large composite textile mills. However, the time series data on registered factories in Ahmedabad between 1977 and 1995 suggested that the number of factories increased consistently. The number of workers, however, increased between 1977 and 1987 and more or less stagnated thereafter. The closure of large production mills was partly compensated by the emergence of a much larger number of smaller units. Decentralization and specialization of the production process, partly fueled by support from various Government agencies and financial institutions, probably explain this increase in the number of units. This reflects the industrial dynamism of the city (Unni and Uma Rani 2000).

The stagnation in organized manufacturing employment has been largely due to the decline of the textile industry in which a large proportion of workers was employed in the seventies. Although some large textile mills closed down in the 1980s, the absolute number of textile industrial units has, in fact, increased. Absolute number and proportion of workers in the registered textile units, however, declined sharply during 1977 to 1987 and slowly thereafter until 1995. The industries that gained importance during this period were manufacturing of rubber, plastic, petroleum and coal products, machinery, machine tools and parts, and basic metals and alloys. These groups of industries constituted nearly half of the registered units in the city (46%) and 31% of the employment in 1995.

Garment Industry

There has been substantial growth in the unorganized segment of the manufacturing sector in Ahmedabad. In fact, most of the garment units and workers were situated in the unorganized or informal sector as we shall see below. The garment industry in Ahmedabad operates within a segmented market. The segmentation is in terms of organization of production, size of units, area of concentration of manufacturing activity, products manufactured, and the markets to which it caters. Broadly, there are three segments in this market. The top-most segment is the large factory sector, the second is the small units and shops, and the third is the home-based garment workers.

All factories employing 10 workers with power or 20 workers without power have to be registered under the Indian Factories Act, 1948. They constitute the formal or organized segment of the garment industry. In our fieldwork, however, we observed that there were many small units that had not obtained registration and were hence apprehensive to talk to us. Information on the number of factories registered and the number of workers in them are available with the Chief Inspector of Factories and at the country level are published in the Annual Survey of Industries. The published data is available only at the level of the Gujarat state. However, we were able to obtain data for the city of Ahmedabad for three years, in the 1970s, 1980s, and 1990s (Table 6.2).

NIC code 26 refers to the manufacture of all textile products. Manufacture of garments alone can be obtained only at the three-digit level of the industry code. This was not available to us. The Chief Inspector of Factories reported only 127 units manufacturing all textile products in 1995–96 and employing 3,179 workers. Obviously the number of registered units in the garment sector alone would be even smaller; about 55 in 1999.

The growth of the garment industry in this sector is also very minimal. The number of registered factories grew from 70 in 1977, to 91 in 1987–88, and to 127 in 1995–96, for an annual exponential growth of 2.6% in the first period and 3.3% in the second period. The number of workers engaged in this sector rose from 1,559 to 1972 to 3,197

Table 6.2   Estimates of Enterprises and Employment in the Formal/Registered Garment Industry in Ahmedabad City

	Number of Units		Number of Workers		Average Size of Units
1977	70	(4.25)	1,559	(0.96)	22.3
1987–88	91	(3.16)	1,972	(1.05)	21.7
1995–96	127	(2.48)	3,197	(1.77)	25.2

Notes: Estimates refer to National Industrial Classification (NIC) code 26 including manufacture of all textile products.
Figures in parentheses refer to percentage of all workers and units in the registered manufacturing industry.
Source: Annual Survey of Industries and Chief Inspector of Factories, Ahmedabad.

during the three years, for an exponential growth rate of 2.3% and 6.9% respectively in the two periods. It appears that only the very large factories are registered and the small workshops employing more than 10 workers are not included in these estimates.

Small factories and shops, many of which probably employ more than 10 workers and avoid the registration under the Factories Act, form this second segment. These units engage between 5 to 15 or more workers. They operate in large rooms with a number of sewing machines around which the workers are organized. The workers are mostly engaged on piece-rate wages. Here again the majority of workers are women.

These units manufacture mainly shirts, pants, midi-skirts, bermudas, frocks, and gowns. Some units exclusively manufacture school uniforms. These units cater to two kinds of markets. The better quality products, bermudas, shirts, frocks, and gowns are meant for the national level markets, mainly Bombay, Delhi, and Calcutta. A large segment of bermudas and other products are sold in Bombay. These products are also subcontracted out by the large well-known garment shopping chains in Ahmedabad city. The lower quality products ("chalu maal" in local terminology) are meant for the local market in Ahmedabad and are sold by local shops and vendors in the walled area of the city. This segment of the garment industry also caters to the regional market such as small towns and rural areas of Gujarat.

Most of these units obtain their orders from large merchants and operate as sub-contract units. Here we are likely to find a chain of subcontractors down which the raw material passes and up which the final products find their way to the final market. It would be interesting to observe how value is added to the product at various stages and what share of this value added is actually obtained by the women workers at the bottom of this chain.

The official data collection machinery collects data on this unorganized or informal segment in its Unorganized Sector Surveys conducted by the National Sample Survey Organization, Government of India. We were able to obtain data on this segment of the industry for the urban areas of Ahmedabad district, namely Ahmedabad city for the year 1994–95 when this data was last collected. The National Industrial Classification code 26, all textile products, was estimated to consist of 12,157 units employing 34,478 workers. The specific three-digit industry group 265 consists of garment units alone. This segment was estimated to consist of 2,237 units employing 5,967 workers in 1994–95. Of these workers 5,005, or 84%, were women (Table 6.3).

The home-based garment workers form the bottom-most layer of this industry. The term "home-based worker" is used for two types of workers who carry out remunerative work within their homes. They are independent, own-account workers and dependent subcontract workers. The term "homeworker" is used to designate the second category of dependent workers only. The International Labor Organization (ILO) Home Work Convention clearly defines a homeworker as a person who carries out work for remuneration in the premises of his/her choice, other than the workplace of the employer, resulting in a product or service as specified by the employer, irrespective

Table 6.3   Estimates of Enterprises and Employment in the Informal Sector Garment Industry in Ahmedabad City

	Units	Workers		
		Male	Female	Total
Small Factories/ Workshops (1994-95)	2237	962	5,005	5,966
Home-based Workers (1998)	—	7,800	27,157	34,957

Estimates refer to NIC code 265, only manufacture of garments and apparel.

Sources: NSS, Unorganized Manufacturing Sector Survey, Unpublished Data and Kantor, 1999, Home-based Garment Workers.

of who provided the equipment, material, or inputs used. This segment of the garment industry operates mainly through contractors. These contractors take the material from the large merchants or shops and supply it to home-based workers in the city. They collect the finished product and return it to the supplier for final sale in the market. The home-based workers are almost 100% women. The cloth merchants are mainly concentrated in the cloth markets of the city. This segment manufactures mainly frocks for children, petticoats, and gowns, which are much lower quality products, are meant for the local market, and are sold in the small retail outlets. This segment also becomes active during the festival season. These women garment home-based workers are also likely to work through a chain of contractors and subcontractors. This is particularly true since the women are located at a distance and are spread out over vast areas in the city and even in some semi-urban locations.

We made an independent estimate of these home-based garment workers in Ahmedabad city (Kantor 1999). The estimates were obtained by inflating by the inverse of the sampling fraction the number of home-based garment workers found through a one stage stratified cluster sampling design. The 43 wards of Ahmedabad city were stratified into four strata according to subjective information about varying concentration of home-based garment workers. The four strata included areas of very high, high, standard, and low concentration of such workers. Areas based on grouped census blocks were created within the four strata. Areas within each stratum were chosen randomly, separately for men and women. These selected areas were enumerated in search of home-based garment workers. This enumeration resulted in an estimation of home-based garment workers of 34,957 for Ahmedabad city. Of them, 27,157 were women garment workers, that is, nearly 78% of the workers (see Table 6.3).

Subcontracting Chains of Garment Manufacturing

The following three cases of subcontracting chains are from different segments of the garments industry in Ahmedabad city. The first case is of a small shop that subcontracts garment making to home-based workers. The second case is a small factory/unit and the third is of a large factory. These three cases represent the three segments of the garment industry discussed above.

Case 1: Ready-made Shop/Subcontractor to Home-based Workers

The ready-made garment shop, Punam Garments, was run by a 34-year old widow. She operated as a subcontractor, wholesaler and retailer. She bought the cloth from the cloth mills in the city. The garment making was subcontracted out to home-based garment workers on a piece-rate basis. The products were low quality garments mainly catering to consumers in small towns, rural areas, local shops, and footpath vendors in the city. Such ready-made garment shops constituted one of the most common and simplest forms of subcontracting chains in the garment industry.

The value addition involved in the manufacture of a half sleeve "kurta" (traditional shirt) of size 28 inches was computed. The final product was sold to the consumer by a wholesaler or retailer (other than our respondent) at approximately Rs.50 per piece. The cost of the cloth was about 28% of the final price of the product. The garment was cut by a "cutting master" who visited the shop every alternate day and was paid on a piece-rate basis. The stitching, attaching of buttons, etc. and ironing of the final product was done by different home-based workers. While the "cutting master" and "garment maker" obtained about 3% each, the person attaching buttons received about 1.5% of the price of the product. Punam Garments obtained only about 4.5% of the value addition. The rest of the 60% of the value added was absorbed as the wholesaler and retailer margins. Obviously, the worst-off in the chain were the women home-based workers.

Case 2: Small Factory/Subcontracting Unit

The second case is of a subcontracting garment unit manufacturing the "salwaar kameez," a popular traditional Indian ladies garment. This unit was run by a subcontractor along with his brother who helped in the supervision of the workers. About 21 workers were employed in the unit, of whom were nine tailors, two "cutting masters," one ironing man, five people doing embroidery work, three helpers, and one supervisor. Four of the employees were women. The subcontractor himself was a tailor before he established this unit. The unit was four years old.

The small factory operated as a subcontracting unit. It obtained its cloth from the agents who bought the material at the cloth markets in the cities of Ahmedabad and Surat. Cotton fabric was obtained from Ahmedabad, while synthetic fabric was from Surat. These agents provided the design and pattern for the garment to the subcontracting unit. The garment was cut, stitched, decorated with embroidery work, ironed, and packed in the unit studied. Sometimes the ironing was subcontracted out to an ironing man. The agent picked up the garment when it was ready and delivered it to the cloth merchants. Wholesalers and retailers approached the cloth merchants for these garments that then reached the final consumer.

The final product is sold for about Rs.400–500. Of course, the garments with more embroidery work as well as of better fabric would fetch better prices and margins. The cost of the cloth was about 25% of the price of the final product. The value addition in garment making at the subcontractors unit was about 25% as well. However, the stitching of the garment cost only about 2% of the market value of the garment. The wholesaler or retailer margin was about 15%. This adds to about 65% of the value added of the product. The rest, 35% of the price of the product, was absorbed by various middlemen, agents, subcontractors, etc. Here again the workers obtained very little of the benefits of this production activity.

Case 3: Medium-sized Factory/Subcontracting Unit

The third case is of a relatively large, medium-sized (in the industry parlance) garment unit. This unit hired about 100 workers, of whom more than 50 were women. The unit manufactured jeans made out of denim fabric as well as cotton trousers for men. The jeans produced were of the brand "logo." The unit obtained the fabric from a couple of very large textile mills that produced a very large proportion of the denim fabric in the country. The garment was manufactured within the subcontracted unit in an assembly line production system. The washing of the jeans, part of the finishing process, was subcontracted out to a nearby unit. The final product was packed and sent back to the mill. The mill then sold the product to the consumers through its authorized distributors and retail outlets.

The final product was sold at about Rs.500. The cost of the fabric was about 30% of the market value of the final product. The value addition for the making of the garment at the subcontracting unit was about 15% of the value of the product. The washing of the jeans added another 7% to the value of the jeans. The distributors and agents had a margin of about 8%. The final retailer's margin was the rest, about 40% of the value added of the product. It is difficult to calculate the share of an individual worker in the value of the product since about 35 workers were involved in the assembly line production of a pair of jeans. However, the share of each individual worker was relatively small in the overall value added.

A comparison of the three cases provides interesting insights. The case of the lowest segment in the garment industry is represented by case one. It is the simplest chain with very few layers. The second case is of the middle segment of the small factory or workshops. This has the most complex chain with many layers of agents and middlemen. These agents obtain about 40% of the value addition of the product. The third case is of the relatively upper segment of the garment market. This is a very organized segment where most of the value addition is retained by the cloth manufacturer. The distribution and retailing also more or less remains within the company because the product is branded. The cost of the cloth takes up 25 to 30% of the value of the product in all three cases. The share of the individual worker remains very small, about 2–3% of the value of the product in all the cases, though this is not very clear in the last case of assembly line production.

WOMEN SUBCONTRACTED WORKERS

This research was essentially aimed at analyzing the working conditions of women as subcontract workers in the garment industry. The impact of their work on their lives and gender roles in the household and in society are analyzed below. The empirical part of the study was based on a survey of 114 women and 70 men and focus group discussions (FGD) separately with factory workers and home-based women workers. The survey was limited to workers in small, unorganized units or workshops. Thus we have concentrated on the lower segment of the garment industry where, as we observed earlier, the majority of the units and workers are concentrated.

Age and Education

The women workers in the small garment units in our survey were relatively young. About 56% of them were below the age of 25, with 36% between the age of 15 and 20. Only about 21% of the male workers were below the age of 20. This was reflected in their marital status, with about 45% of the women workers being unmarried. Only 37% of the men were unmarried. In fact, what was more striking was that while 63% of the men were currently married, only 45% of the women were so. A small proportion of the women in these units were widowed (7%) and divorced (4%). None of the male workers reported themselves to be in the latter statuses. This implies that some of these women started this work in the factories due to the compulsion to earn their own living after divorce or widowhood. There was a distinct difference in the some of the characteristics of these two FGD groups. The factory workers were young, almost all between the ages of 18 to 30. The home-based women were more mixed and consisted of a large number of older women between the ages of 30 to 55.

The level of education of the workers was quite low. The women workers were in general worse off than the men in their educational attainments. About 9% of the women were illiterate as compared with about 6% of the men. A higher proportion of men had completed secondary school as well as attended college. However, a slightly higher proportion of women had completed higher secondary school compared to the men. The educational levels of the women in the FGDs revealed that the factory workers were more likely to have studied beyond the primary school level, compared to the home-based women. This was also partly due to the religious composition of the two groups, as we shall see below.

Ethnic Composition

The majority of the men and women workers in the small factories belonged to Hindu households. However, the interesting difference was that while nearly 19% of the men belonged to Muslim households, only about 8% of the women were Muslim. This was in spite of the fact that a large proportion of the Muslim population in the old city areas of Ahmedabad, where the garment units are located, was not very well off.

The Muslims were, however, engaged in the garment industry in the form of home-based workers. They were particularly involved in embroidering and sewing other ornamental items on the "salwar kurtas," a traditional dress of Indian women. We had observed this in an earlier study of the informal sector in Ahmedabad (Unni 2000) and also in our focus group discussions with home-based women workers. The three groups of factory workers in the FGDs did not have any Muslim women. However, two of the groups in the FGDs with home-based workers consisted entirely of Muslim women. The third group of home-based workers was a mixed group with a few Muslim women. Obviously these women faced social and cultural restrictions on their mobility that made them seek home-based work.

Another interesting fact was that among the Hindu households, of both the male and female workers, about 45% belonged to the lower caste groups. The women belonged to both the scheduled and backward caste groups, whereas a large proportion of the men were of the backward caste groups. In the social hierarchy, the scheduled castes form the lowest strata of the Hindu society, followed by the scheduled tribes and backward castes.

There is a clear social stratification of the workers in this sector. The workers in the informal (unorganized) sector belong mainly to the lower end of the social hierarchy. Muslim women, faced with a double disadvantage of socio-cultural barriers to mobility and poverty, were found to prefer home-based work.

Employment Status of the Worker and Family Members

The majority of the garment workers, both men and women, were casual workers (Table 6.4). That is, getting either daily or piece-rate wages. About 40% of the fathers or husbands of the women workers were salaried workers. Almost 35% of the husbands were casual workers, along with a smaller proportion of the fathers. As we shall see below, the earnings of these husbands and fathers were quite low, necessitating the work of their daughters and wives in such low paying activities. Only a small proportion of the fathers and husbands were actually unemployed. In contrast, the overwhelming majority of the wives of the male workers, 82%, were not economically active and were engaged in household duties. The majority of the working wives were, however, casual workers.

Economic Status of the Household

In general, the economic status of the workers in the small garment factories, and the households to which they belonged, was quite low (Table 6.5). At both ends of the distribution, the households to which the men belonged appeared to be worse off than the households to which the women belonged. While about 23% of the men's households earned monthly incomes below Rs.1500, about 15% of the households of women workers did so.

Table 6.4　Employment Status of the Worker and Family Members

Employment Status	Female Workers			Male Workers		
	Self	Father	Husband	Self	Father	Wife
Salaried	34.2	41.3	40.8	35.7	38.5	2.6
Casual Labor	60.5	26.1	34.7	60.0	11.5	10.3
Self-employed	4.4	10.9	18.4	2.8	20.3	2.6
Unemployed	—	6.5	4.1	—	3.8	—
Household Work	—	—	—	—	—	82.1
Old/ Disabled	—	—	—	—	26.9	—
Other	—	15.3	2.0	—	—	2.6
All	100.0	100.0	100.0	100.0	100.0	100.0
	(114)	(46)	(49)	(70)	(26)	(39)

At the other end, about 14% of the male worker households earned monthly incomes above Rs.5000 while about 18% of the female worker households did so.

The reverse was however true for the workers themselves. The women workers earned much lower incomes than the male workers in the small garment factories in our sample. About 76% of the women earned less than Rs.1500 per month, while only 34% of the men earned such low incomes. At the other end of the distribution, only about 3.5% of the women workers earned more than Rs.2000 per month, whereas about 34% of the men did so. This could be a reflection of the division of labor within the garment factories and the kind of work that the women did compared to the men. The men were more often engaged as supervisors on a monthly income than women. The men also undertook the cutting and tailoring of men's garments such as pants and shirts, which had much higher piece-rate wages.

Some of the women in the FGDs were sole breadwinners in the households. The income levels of the households ranged from Rs.2000–5000 per month. Some of the factory workers had even higher incomes. However, the household income levels of the home-based workers were somewhat lower, ranging from Rs.100 to 4000 per month. In general, the households to which these women belonged were very poor. However, the men workers belonged to even poorer households. This probably reflected the fact that the women were less likely to be the sole earners in the households. The opposite was true of the workers themselves, with the women earning much lower incomes compared to the men. An economic stratification of the workers in the garment industry existed as well, with women workers in the small factories appearing to earn the most, followed by the small factory workers, and the lowest earning accruing to the home-based workers.

Table 6.5   Monthly Incomes of Worker, Family Members and the Household

Income (Rs)	Female Worker			
	Self	Father	Husband	Household
<1000	28.9	23.4	20.4	—
1000–1500	47.4	27.7	34.7	7.0
1500–2000	20.2	19.4	30.6	7.9
2000–2500	3.5	8.5	6.1	15.0
2500–5000	—	17.0	6.1	52.2
5000–10000	—	4.2	2.0	14.3
10000	—	—	—	3.6
All	100.0 (114)	100.0 (47)	100.0 (49)	100.0 (114)

Income (Rs)	Male Worker			
	Self	Father	Wife	Household
<1000	7.2	61.5	97.4	1.4
1000–1500	27.1	7.7	—	7.1
1500–2000	31.5	23.1	—	14.3
2000–2500	18.6	—	—	18.6
2500–5000	15.7	7.7	2.6	44.3
5000–10000	—	—	—	14.3
>10000	—	—	—	—
All	100 (70)	100.0 (26)	100.0 (39)	100.0 (70)

Previous Employment

A large proportion of the workers were engaged in the manufacture of garments before they joined this particular unit. About 72% of the women and 60% of the men reported working in the garment industry in other units before joining this one. About 50% of the women and men had been working in the current unit for 1–4 years. However, 48% of the women and 24% of the men had worked in other units for less than 4 years. Thus, a large proportion of the workers were relatively recent entrants into the garment manufacturing activity. There was a considerable turnover of employment in this sector, particularly among the women. A larger proportion of the men had worked for longer years in both the current and other units in garment manufacturing. This might, of course, reflect the age profile of the workers, with a large proportion of the women being younger and new entrants.

In the FGDs we also found that women were either engaged in household work or in stitching and tailoring activities at home before undertaking the current work. Many of the younger girls in the factories were new entrants to the labor force. Only a few home-based garment workers said they had been undertaking bidi-rolling or agarbatti-making earlier.

We did not observe any drastic change in the labor market due to the growth of the garment industry in Ahmedabad. Most of the women were young and new recruits into this industry. This partly reflects the new units set up in recent years and also the preference for young workers in the factories. In spite of the seemingly low incomes earned in this sector, the wages were higher than that obtained in some of the traditional industries such as bidi-rolling and agarbatti-making. Besides, this activity can also be undertaken at home. This is the reason for the shift reported by some of the older home-based women to garment making.

Sexual Division of Labor in the Garment Work

There was a clear division of the type of garments stitched by women and men. Among the workers stitching ready-made garments, only about 12% of the women stitched men's pants and shirts, while 36% of the men did so. The majority of the women made dresses and hosiery (27 and 29% respectively). Only 18% and 24% of the men made these two types of garments. A large number of the men did not undertake the actual stitching in any case.

The men were also engaged in the supervision of the work, cutting and allocation of the work, and in other activities such as procuring orders, marketing, etc. There were very few women supervisors. The women engaged in minor activities such as cutting the loose threads left over, stitching the buttons and the other finishing, and ornamentation work. This explains the lower piece-rates obtained by the women and the overall lower monthly incomes they earned. It seems the sexual division of labor at home was carried over to the work place as well.

Some women in the FGDs among factory workers felt that there was a distinct difference in the garments sewed by men and women workers. Women sewed only "salwar suits," pyjamas, and children's clothes, while trousers were sewn only by men. Some women said that customers and subcontractors would not prefer trousers and shirts sewn by women. Women in the larger factories were involved in the "finishing" activities. "Cutting" work was also only done by men. Men consequently earned much higher wages per day. The older women felt that there was no particular reason for this except tradition. It was interesting that some of the younger women in our FGDs with the larger factory workers felt that there was no preference as such for male workers. The employer was only interested in good quality work and was not concerned whether the worker was male or female. However, men had a distinct advantage of being able to do overtime in case of need, while women could not do so.

A form of social and economic stratification, as observed in the society, was reflected in the ethnic composition and economic position of the women workers in the garment industry. Similarly, the women also faced stratification in the division of labor. That is, the so-called "women's" activities and women's garments were entrusted to them. All these activities had the label of being less skilled. The skilled "cutting" work was mainly entrusted to the men.

EFFECT OF SUBCONTRACT WORK ON ROLE AND POSITION IN THE HOUSEHOLD

Change in Household Incomes and Expenditures

The impact of the subcontract work on the economic position of the household was sought to be judged through some direct questioning in the survey. About 48% of the women and 51% of the men workers said that their household incomes had increased since they started this work. About 5% of the women and 1% of the men said that their incomes had decreased since they took up this work. It is likely that they were employed in more remunerative activities before this. However, 42% of the women and 46% of the men also said that there was no change in their incomes.

The workers were asked if there was any change in the pattern of expenditure of the household since they undertook this work. Twenty-four percent of both men and women said there was a change. Most of these workers said they were able to satisfy the needs of the household members, and a small proportion, 1% of men and 3% of women, said they saved money for their marriage. About 8% of the women said they had some money to spend on their own needs due to this work. Obviously the men never felt this was a constraint since they were earners in any case, hence only 1% reported this.

Role in Decision-making

It is generally hypothesized that the participation of women in economic activities leads to an improved role in decision-making within the household. In the survey we asked a direct question to the workers regarding decision-making in the household. Only about 10.5% of the men and women said that they took household decisions alone. A large proportion of the women said that the household decisions were taken by their parents. This directly reflects the fact that a large proportion of these women were young, unmarried, and lived with their parents. This proportion was lower among the men. The most striking result from the gender perspective was that 25% of the women workers said that they took the decision together with their husbands. Only about 10% of the men said so. In a direct question on whether the workers felt that there was any increase in decision-making power since taking up subcontracted work,

36% of the women and 38% of the men responded positively. Thus participation in work did seem to make a difference to the decision-making powers of the women, particularly if they were married.

In the FGDs it was noted that the decision-making power of women had increased with the entry into this work, but important decisions such as marriage alliances were still decided by the men.

Another aspect of empowerment is the capacity to spend one's own earnings and undertake the household expenditures. In order to understand this, we asked a direct question on who actually spends the money earned from this subcontracted work (Table 6.6). The empowerment of the women was clearer here with 38% of the women and 34% of the men saying that they spend their earnings themselves. However, noting the young age of our female respondents, about 51% of them also said that they handed over their earnings to their parents who spend the money. Among men, 44% said that the spending was undertaken by other family members.

Finally, we also tried to see if there was a difference in the way the money was spent, or the items of expenditure incurred by the women and men workers. Due to multiple uses of the earnings it was difficult to obtain clear answers regarding the specific items of expenditure. However, some clear differences in the expenditure patterns of the men and women were observed. Almost all the earnings of the women workers were spent on the household and childcare. About 19% of the men workers clearly stated that they spent the money on themselves. Another 31% of the men said they spent the money on items that could not be included in household expenditures. Obviously, the responsibility of the women is totally towards the household irrespective of her marital status, while this was not universally true for the men.

In the FGDs the women said that most of the income was spent on food and rent for the house. Anything between 10 to 90% of the husband's income was reported to be available for household expenditures.

Table 6.6   Persons Spending Earnings

Person Who Spends Earnings	Women Workers	Men Workers
Self	37.7	34.3
Husband / Wife	4.4	—
Parents	50.9	21.4
Spouses Together	—	—
Other Family Members	6.2	44.3
No response	—	—
All	100.0 (114)	100.0 (70)

Wages in the subcontracted work in the garment industry are low, but still above many of the locally available jobs. Hence, participation in this activity leads to improved incomes for the households. Some of the women who reported a decrease in incomes were probably formerly engaged in the textile mills (organized sector), which closed down. While most of these women workers belonged to poor households, the fact of being engaged in an economic activity did lead to some empowerment for the women. Many of the decisions were taken in consultation with the women, though crucial decisions were still taken by the men. An almost similar proportion of men and women reported being able to spend their earnings themselves. The rest pooled their resources together with the rest of the family, which is quite common in the Indian context of joint family systems.

Time Allocation and Household Work

In order to capture the gender allocation of household work, we canvassed a series of questions on the time spend in household duties, personal care, economic work and time of waking up to all respondents.

Wake Up Hours

As expected, most of the women woke up earlier than the men. About 63% of the women woke up on or before 6:00 A.M. In contrast, nearly 50% of the men reported waking up only at or after 8:00 A.M. This is a luxury afforded only to the men even in the relatively not so well to do households.

Time Allocation

The gender roles of the workers clearly conform to the expected norms when we study the time allocation in the household. The women spend more hours at the home in household duties, while the men spend more time at work. Most women engaged in economic activities for only 8 or less than 8 hours. Only 27% of the women compared to 66% of the men spent more than 8 hours in economic activities.

Most of the women workers were involved in household duties of cleaning, cooking and childcare. Among the male workers, only 8.6% spent time on house cleaning, 7.2% said they cooked, and 15.7% said they looked after children. The other major differences in the time allocation by gender were that the men spent more time than women in personal care and entertainment, and got more hours of sleep.

Thus the classic gender roles were performed even in the households where the women were working. The women however, took on fewer hours of economic activities in order to fulfil their role. They also took less time off for themselves or to sleep in order to undertake the household duties. It was not apparent that subcontracted work was changing any gender roles for most women. A few men did, however, report to be performing some of the household duties as well.

When the women were asked if they received any help from family members in the household duties, 17.5% said that they got help in cleaning, 16.7% in cooking, 2.6% in childcare, and 3.5% in other activities. This help was mainly from the other female members of the households.

In the FGDs, all the women reported that that they had the dual responsibility of work and household work. Most of the women said that there was no relief from household work. Only the unmarried women had some relief from household responsibilities. Childcare was however, shared by the mother-in-law, husband, and sometimes by the neighbors. Some of the husbands helped to buy the provisions and performed other tasks outside the household. However, it was categorically stated that the men never entered the kitchen. All women in all the FGDs clearly stated that the men had more time to relax and socialize with friends.

Organization

Most of the policy initiatives discussed earlier and the efforts being made are for the large manufacturers of garments. Of course, due to the subcontracting chains through which this industry operates, these will also be beneficial to the smaller units. But for the large mass of units in the small factory segment, the focus of this research, and the women subcontracted workers, it is not clear how all these initiatives and efforts will affect them. Some forms of organization of the small units are necessary to enable them to survive in the new scenario that may emerge after 2002. Some associations of the garment manufacturers and the large trade union Self Employed Women's Association (SEWA) in Ahmedabad, and their strategies are discussed below.

Garment Manufacturers Association

There are a number of Garment Manufacturers Associations in Ahmedabad. The "Sindhi Market Kapad Mahajan Association" is very old, while the "Ahmedabad Punjabi Suits Association" was formed in the last 5 years. Five years ago there were a handful of shops dealing in wholesale of "Punjabi-Suits" (a popular women's garment), in the price range of Rs.50 to Rs.5000. But now there are thousands of such shops, which cater to the national and international markets (mainly Singapore, Dubai, Europe, and the United States). Only two of three shops, however, have export licenses. The rest of the shop owners who export Punjabi suits operate through "commission agents" (such agents are commonly known as "*adatiya*" and are people who collect the garments, put the "*nada*" in the pyjamas, finish the garments, and send them to the exporters for export. These agents operate at a margin of 2%). The shopkeeper deals with these agents and the billing of garment sold is made in the names of these "commission agents."

There are about 300 members in the Ahmedabad Punjabi Suits Association and 1,000 members in the Sindhi Market Kapad Mahajan Association. These associations are not very active but were formed to have a collective voice. Problems such as sales tax, octroi, payment delays, etc., are addressed together. But on a day-to-day basis, fabric and garment dealers (most of whom receive garments manufactured by subcontractors) do not have anything to do with the association. Every dealer goes about his own business on his own.

In an interview, Mr. P. Keshwani, Joint Secretary of Ahmedabad Punjabi Suits Association and Sindhi Market Kapad Mahajan Association, emphasized that the associations were not active at all. He also emphasized that when the Government imposes high tax and octroi structures it creates more corruption among the shop owners and manufacturers, who, for example, do not then mention all sales in their account books. The Punjabi Suits Association and Sindhi Market Kapad Mahajan Association were instrumental in convincing the Government to reduce the octroi rates from a hiked 2% to 1.5%. Since unstitched cloth does not have any sales tax (the present sales tax rate on garments is 2%), many of the shop owners sell "unstitched cloth" (punjabi suit dress material), which caters to small towns and rural areas.

There is also a "Handloom Association" with about 200 members. In the past, there was no taxation for handloom items or on textile products of less than Rs.100 value. Now there is a sales tax on these items. Thus, some shop owners who sold handicraft items and textile products of value less than Rs.100 decided to form the "Handloom Association." The "Gujarat Garments Association" has about 300 to 400 members. Forty to fifty of the members own large garment manufacturing units. This association represents Gujarat at the fashion trade expositions organized at Delhi, Mumbai, Bangalore, etc.

Many garment shop owners are members of more than one association. It appears that these associations are formed with a specific objective in mind and are generally inactive otherwise. Most of these associations consist of traders rather than of the manufacturing units. This is an important form of organizing for the small manufacturing and trading units and can be used effectively to negotiate with the Government. However, it remains to be seen how this form of organizing can be helpful in the face of competition from large manufacturers and foreign brand names.

Organizing Strategy of SEWA

SEWA (Self Employed Women's Association) organizes self-employed women to achieve their goals of full employment and self-reliance through the joint strategies of struggle and development. Through struggle, women build the collective strength needed to ensure that they are treated fairly and equitably by employers and Government officials. Through development, they work to create their own economic institutions, generate new employment opportunities, build their financial assets, and obtain vital social security benefits such as health care and childcare.

SEWA's Strategy in the Garment Industry

SEWA recognizes that the garment industry is segmented. The three segments are similar to those we identified: 1) Large factories that are registered under the Indian Factories Act and are in the organized sector; 2) Small factories and workshops on an average employing 5–15 workers; and 3) Home-based garment workers.

In an earlier phase of organization, SEWA concentrated on the large factory sector. There was no record in the factories of who the workers were or how many years they had been working. SEWA demanded Identity Cards (ID) for the workers, which would make it easier for them to organize and campaign for minimum wage and social security benefits and ensure they are counted as workers, nationally. The struggle continued for some time. The factories finally issued ID cards and within a week closed down the factory. The unit was merged with another unit and work was resumed in another name on other premises. The union workers attached to SEWA were not given any further work. SEWA filed cases and struggled for many years. After this setback in the struggle, SEWA temporarily stopped working in the large factory segment.

The large factories now hire a number of contractors, often "dummy" contractors, and split up the workers in the factory into small groups of 11–15 workers. They operate on the same premises. The Chief Inspector of Factories, under whose office the factories are registered, visits the factories for inspection. SEWA members are also invited to join the inspection. However, the factory owners claim that the workers are working under independent contractors. In this way they are able to avoid giving a number of benefits to the workers. Of course, one cannot rule out collusion between the owners and the officials. The experience of SEWA has been that during inspections, if an innocent worker reports the number of years he/she has been working in the factory or provides any other information, he/she is given no further work from the next day.

SEWA would like to now concentrate on the informal sector. It has a large membership in the home-based worker segment. In the small factory segment, however, it is difficult to unionize. Workers are afraid to join any organization because the moment the factory owner or contractor comes to know of this he does not give any further work to the worker. This was also observed when we attempted to conduct the survey of women workers reported earlier.

SEWA is currently conducting a campaign for Minimum Wages and ID cards for the workers. The Minimum Wage in the garment industry is currently Rs.60.6 per dozen garments irrespective of the type of garment. Of course, most workers in the informal sector do not receive these wages.

ISSUES FOR ORGANIZATION

On what issues is it best to organize the workers? Some issues that need to be brought into focus, through campaigns and struggle, are highlighted below.

1. Minimum Wages: The minimum wage has been fixed recently for garment workers at Rs.60.6 per dozen garments under the Minimum Wages Act. The issues here are whether this is adequate and how to ensure that a majority of the workers receive this wage. This is particularly true for the small factory sector and more so for the home-based workers. In addition, high wages alone are not enough to sustain livelihoods. Some norm for the minimum days of employment in the year is also required. We observed that a minimum norm of 250 days is not met for most workers in the garment industry, particularly for women.

2. Identity Cards: Minimum wage regulation by itself does not guarantee that the worker receives the specified wage. The worker has to prove that he is a worker in that industry. This is true for all the segments in the garment industry because even the large factories do not provide the workers with any written contracts or documents. This problem is, of course, most acute for the home-based workers. This raises the issue of identity cards for the workers in order to avail of any of the benefits that should accrue to them. A related issue is whether ID cards should be issued by industry/trade or by category of work, such as home-based workers or vendors, etc., or simply as workers. This issue arises because of the seasonal nature of work. A worker may make garments in one season and make kites in another season. Similarly, vendors may hawk different commodities in different seasons. However, since most regulations are trade based it might be necessary to issue ID cards based on trades.

3. Welfare Fund or Social Security: The ideal case quoted for the benefits of social security is the Welfare Fund for the bidi (local small cigarette) workers. Bidi-making is a well-regulated trade because it is very old and a specific law, the Bidi and Cigar Workers Act, exists for it. The Welfare Fund is regulated by a Tripartite Body consisting of Government, employers, and worker's representatives. ID cards are provided to the workers. They receive minimum wages. Education of children is supported through scholarships and money for uniforms for their children, costs of hospitalization are met, insurance in case of sudden death, and travel for recreation for the worker are among the benefits received. However, provident fund/pension is not included and this issue has been taken up. A similar fund for the garment workers, agarbatti workers, and for contract labor is under discussion.

National Level Legislation

Much national level legislation exists, such as the Minimum Wages Act, Provident Fund Act, Employees' State Insurance for health, etc. The problem concerns the coverage of this legislation, which generally extends only to workers in certain trades in the case of Minimum Wages and only to the formal sector in other cases. In general, the informal sector workers, particularly the home-based workers, are left out of most legislation even when it exists, although certain states have extended the Provident Fund to include certain categories of informal sector workers.

The invisibility of these workers is what works against them, and the issuance of Identity Cards for the workers therefore becomes crucial. Legislation that accepts that all workers require an ID card, including the modus-operandi of how and to whom such cards will be issued, would go a long way toward promoting the organization and campaign for minimum wages and social security benefits for workers.

The question of how to fund such Social Security benefits also needs to be answered. The case of the bidi workers welfare fund is successful because it is financed through a cess or tax on the commodity. Similar options for the benefits of other workers must be devised.

CONCLUSIONS

In recent years there has been a disintegration of the production process and a consequent rise in subcontracting. Subcontracting is a change in the Fordist pattern of the division of labor associated with mass production. This disintegration of the production process towards subcontracting can be conceptualized as occurring due to pull or push factors. The defining feature of the pull towards subcontracting is its productivity-enhancing nature. In contrast to the pull towards subcontracting, firms can be pushed into outsourcing because of increasing economic costs, high levels of competition, or in order to circumvent labor legislation (Balakrishnan and Huang 2000). There is evidence of increase in subcontracting arrangements between firms in India, which could be both push and pull in nature. The form of subcontracting we have observed in the garment industry in Ahmedabad, at the lower end of the market segment and in much of home-based work, is an example of the push into subcontracting. At the lower end of the market spectrum, it is lower cost rather than quality that is the determining criterion for capturing market share. This is perhaps what we observed in the small factory segment in Ahmedabad.

There are tremendous prospects for the garment industry in India. India is one of the largest cotton producers in the world. Cotton fabric is slowly becoming very popular even in Europe, the United States, Canada, etc. These countries are becoming more and more conscious of the fact that any fabric which comes into direct contact with the skin should preferably be made of natural fibers. Also, the "eco-friendly" concept is quickly catching on, as is the concept of wrinkle-free trousers for which superior cotton fibers are being developed. In addition, certain "handicraft" hand stitched garments will always find a market. India therefore has a great potential for cotton exports and also for garment manufacturing and exporting since the ready-made garment will be cheaper for India to manufacture (compared to the other countries) for the international market.

The garment industry has been growing in India, in both the domestic and foreign markets. Government policies toward the sector are, however, not very encouraging, unlike other developing countries such as Bangladesh. The Ahmedabad garment industry can be very successful since the city has the two basic ingredients for such an industry, i.e., good entrepreneurship skills and a textile base. Bangalore and Delhi are very successful centers of garment manufacturing units. In fact, fabric from Ahmedabad is obtained for the units located in these cities. There are many export-oriented units in these cities. The large garment factories set up by the Arvind and Ashima industrial houses in Ahmedabad are likely to thrive. The small units we studied could be threatened, however, as the large houses and multinationals would produce the same garments with economies of scale. It is unclear what the role of the middlemen would be, since corporations would sublet work directly or indirectly to the home-based garment workers. Such corporations would certainly be offering a better piece-rate to the home-based garment workers as compared to the piece-rates being offered by the local units. It is likely that even garments such as traditional "pyjamas" would be taken up by such corporations as a potential garment to be manufactured.

In our analysis of value chains we found that in all the segments, women workers were not the direct beneficiaries of the growth in the industry. Most of the margins were absorbed by the middlemen and the retailers. The women workers in the larger units and in the top segment obviously received higher wages, but not necessarily all the benefits due to formal sector workers. However, the women gained in many ways. First they gained employment. The home-based activities such as bidi-making (traditional cigarettes) and incense stick rolling were disappearing, and the garment sector has provided them with new opportunities for work. The women also felt that they had more decision-making power. However, the double burden of work continued and women in the traditional society did not really expect this to change in the near future.

The garment industry in Ahmedabad could grow in the current phase of global markets. The cotton textile base of Ahmedabad and the synthetic textiles of Surat, a city south of Ahmedabad, provide the basic raw materials required. With some encouragement from the Government of Gujarat, large units and export houses could be set up in the city. The workers, however, have to be trained to use more sophisticated machines and manufacture higher quality garments. On an experimental basis, the National Institute of Fashion Technology (NIFT), Gandhinagar, Gujarat had imparted basic training in stitching to women from the slums of Ahmedabad. Some such effort on a larger scale, and in collaboration with the industry groups planning to set up units, needs to be made so that the benefits of the growth of this industry accrue to the women workers.

REFERENCES

Banerjee, N. and A.K. Bagchi. 1981. Change and Choice in Indian Industry. K.P. Bagchi and Co. Ltd., Calcutta.

Balakrishnan, R. and M. Huang. 2000. Flexible Workers-Hidden Employers: Gender and Sub-contracting in the Global Economy. Draft report on a research project of the Women's Economic and Legal Rights Program, Washington DC.

Batra, S.L. 1996. *Employment for Women: A Study of Export-Oriented Garment Industry.* New Delhi: Har-Anand Publications.

Chaterjee, S. and R. Mohan. 1993. India's Garment Exports. In *Economic and Political Weekly*, Review of Industry and Management, August 28.

Kantor, P. 1999. Estimating Numbers in Household Industry: The Case of Home-based Garment Makers in Ahmedabad. Mimeo. Ahmedabad,.

Lalbhai, A., S. Lalbhai, and S. Verma. Undated. Indian Textile Industry, Strategy for Achieving Strong Global Presence. Mimeo.

Report of the Committee to Assess and Forecast Skilled Manpower Requirements up to the Year 2000 for the Garment Export Industry. 1991. New Delhi: Ministry of Textiles.

Morris, S., R. Basant, K. Das, K. Ramachandran, and A. Koshy. 1999. Overcoming Constraints to the Growth and Transformation of Small Firms. Mimeo. Ahmedabad: Indian Institute of Management.

Nagraj, R. 1986. Subcontracting in Indian Manufacturing: Analysis, Evidence and Issues. In Working Paper No. 192. Trivandrum: Center for Development Studies.

Nagraj, R. 1999. Subcontracting as a Means of Technology Diffusion: Evidence from Indian Manufacturing. Mimeo. Mumbai: Indira Gandhi Institute of Development Research, April.

Pani, Pranab K. 1999. Inter-Firm Linkages: A Study of Small Scale Enterprises. Thesis submitted to the Fellow Programme in Management at the Indian Institute of Management. Ahmedabad.

Ramaswamy, K.V. 1999. The Search for Flexibility in Indian Manufacturing: New Evidences on Outsourcing Activities. In *Economic and Political Weekly*, Vol. 34, No. 6. February 6.

Ramaswamy, K.V. and G. Gray. 1999. India's Apparel Sector in the Global Economy: Catching Up or Falling Behind. In *Economic and Political Weekly*, Vol. 33, No. 3. January 17.

Unni, Jeemol. 2000. Urban Informal Sector: Size and Income Generation Processes. SEWA-GIDR-ISST-NCAER Report 2. New Delhi: National Council of Applied Economic Research.

Unni, J. and U. Rani. 2000. Employment and Incomes in India: Case of a City Economy. Paper prepared for AIMS: Assessing the Impact of Micro Enterprise Service Project. Mimeo. Cambridge (USA): John F. Kennedy School of Government.

About the Contributors

Radhika Balakrishnan has a Ph.D. in Economics from Rutgers University and is an Associate Professor of Economics at Marymount Manhattan College. She has worked at the Ford Foundation as a program officer in the Asia Regional Program and was previously on the board of the International Association of Feminist Economics. She is currently on the boards of the Religious Consultation for Reproductive Health, Population and Ethics, and the African American Policy Forum. She has published in the field of gender and development. Recent work includes *Good Sex: Feminist Perspectives from the World's Religions* (Rutgers University Press, 2000) co-edited with Patricia Jung and Mary Hunt. She was a team member on *The Progress of the World's Women* (UNIFEM), and authored "Population" in the *Elgar Companion to Feminist Economics*, edited by Janice Peterson and Margaret Lewis.

Namrata Bali is the Secretary of SEWA (Self Employed Women's Association), a registered trade union of informal sector women workers with a membership of over two million women in India. She spent sixteen years in SEWA organizing urban and rural women into handicraft cooperatives, while the last ten years her main responsibility has been as the Director of the SEWA Academy, the organization's main training. She specializes in textile designing and studies in labor and cooperatives, and edits a monthly periodical for young girls. She is a trainer as well as a director of various documentaries made by Video SEWA.

Lourdes Abad Gula has been a National Council member of PATAMABA National Network of Homeworkers (Pambansang Tagapag-ugnay ng mga Manggagawa sa Bahay) since its founding in 1989 and is currently its National Coordinator, in charge of organizing activities and monitoring a membership of 12,000. She has been the chairperson of the PATAMABA Credit Cooperative since 1994 and was the PATAMABA National Project Coordinator from 1989-1996 in charge of project monitoring and evaluation, loan processing, collections, credit policy-making and resource generation. She obtained her secondary education from Camiling Colleges, Tarlac. She was a National Council member, and Chairperson of the Rizal provincial chapter, of KABAPA—Association of the New Filipina (Katipunan ng Bagong Pilipina), 1986-1989. She was a National Council Member of the SIKAP—Association for the Development of Filipino, 1980-1987.

Swarna Jayaweera has a Masters and Doctoral degree from the University of London, was a post-doctoral fellow at Columbia University, New York and has Hon. D. Litt. degrees from the University of Colombo and the Open University of Sri Lanka. She taught in the Universities of Peradeniya and Colombo and was Professor of Education and Department Head of Social Science Education of the University of Colombo. Subsequently, she was UNESCO advisor and UNICEF consultant on the access of women to education in Nepal, and has been a consultant to UN agencies and bilateral agencies in Sri Lanka and in the Asian Region on education and on women's issues. She is one of the founders of the Centre for Women's Research (CENWOR), Sri Lanka, and its Joint Coordinator. She has contributed extensively to books and to local and to international journals on women and on education. She is Emeritus Professor of Education, University of Colombo, a Fellow of the National Academy of Science and is currently a member of the National Education Commission and the National Committee on Women. She is also a Research Fellow of the Faculty of Graduate Studies of the University of Colombo.

Saba Gul Khattak is a Research Fellow and Deputy Director at the Sustainable Development Policy Institute (SDPI), Pakistan, where she heads the SDPI Program on Gender. She works on the crosscurrents between women's issues and state policies. Her broad research interests include issues of governance, feminism and nationalism, and the political economy of development. Her current research focuses on three areas: issues affecting women workers; women, peace and militarization; and the women's movement in Pakistan. She contributes regularly to dialogues on these issues at national and international fora.

Joseph Y. Lim is a professor at the School of Economics, University of the Philippines, Diliman. He obtained his Ph.D. Economics degree from the University of Pennsylvania. His recent writings include "The Macroeconomics of the East Asian Crisis and the Crisis' Implications on Macroeconomic Theory," (The Manchester School, 1999) and "The Effects of the East Asian Crisis on the Employment of Women and Men: The Philippine Case," (*World Development*, 2000).

Rosalinda Pineda Ofreneo obtained the following academic degrees, all from the University of the Philippines in Diliman: Bachelor of Science in Home Economics, major in Family Life and Child Development (1971); Master of Arts in Communication (1979); and Ph.D. in Philippine Studies (1994). She is currently an associate professor at the Women and Development Program, College of Social Work and Community Development at the University of the Philippines, Diliman. Some of her recent publications include: *Renato Constantino: A Life Revisited*, (Foundation for Nationalist Studies, 2001), *Transforming the Mainstream: Building a Gender-Responsive Bureaucracy in the Philippines, 1975-1978*, co-authored with Jurgette A. Honculada, (United Nations Development Fund for Women, Bangkok, 2000), and *Tinig at Kapangyarihan: Mga*

Kuwentong Buhay ng Kababaihang Manggagawa sa Bahay (University of the Philippines Press, 1999); based on her doctoral dissertation. She is co-editor and co-author of *Carrying the Burden of the World: Women Reflecting on the Effects of the Crisis on Women and Girls,* (University of the Philippines Center of Integrative and Development Studies, 1999).

Asad Sayeed has a Ph.D. in Economics from Cambridge University. Presently he is a visiting research fellow at the Applied Economics Research Centre (AERC), Karachi University. Until recently, he was Director of Research at the Pakistan Institute of Labour Education and Research (PILER); an NGO based in Karachi, Pakistan. There he conducted and coordinated research on labor related and macroeconomic issues. He has also worked as Senior Economist with the Social Policy and Development Centre (SPDC), Karachi. There he conducted research on institutional and political economy issues in the delivery of social services in Pakistan. Sayeed's research work is mainly in the area of political economy analysis issues pertaining to developing countries in general and South Asia in particular. He is a vocal critic of neo-liberal liberalization and structural adjustment policies being pursued in the region. His book, *Political Alignments: the State and Industrialization in Pakistan* will soon be published by Oxford University Press. He is a frequent contributor to the Pakistani press and South Asia related websites.

Jeemol Unni is currently an associate professor at the Gujarat Institute of Development Research, Ahmedabad, India. She did her M.Phil. in Applied Economics at the Centre for Development Studies, Trivandrum and a Ph.D. in Economics at the Sardar Patel Institute of Economic and Social Research, Ahmedabad. She has been a visiting fellow at the Economic Growth Center, Yale University, USA and a Senior Research Fellow at the Institute of Social Studies, the Hague, the Netherlands. Her research interests are in issues related to informal sector, labor markets, national income, social sectors, particularly education and social protection. She has worked as a consultant to the World Bank, International Labour Organization's South Asia Multidisciplinary Advisory Team (SAAT), Asian Regional Team for Employment Promotion (ARTEP), and to the NABARD and SIDBI, specialized banks in India. She has been a member of many national and international committees discussing issues related to the informal sector. She actively collaborates with the Self Employed Women's Association (SEWA), Ahmedabad and Women in Informal Employment Globalizing and Organizing (WIEGO), an international coalition of trade unions, NGOs and academics, in addressing issues related to women in the informal sector.

Index

Also from Kumarian Press...

International Development, Environment, Conflict Resolution, Gender Studies, Global Issues, Globalization, Humanitarian Aid, Microfinance, NGOs, Political Economy

Advocacy for Social Justice: A Global Action and Reflection Guide
David Cohen, Rosa de la Vega, Gabrielle Watson for Oxfam America and the Advocacy Institute

Bound: Living in the Globalized World
Scott Sernau

Capitalism and Justice: Envisioning Social and Economic Fairness
John Isbister

Exploring the Gaps: Vital Links Between Trade, Environment and Culture
James R. Lee

Inequity in the Global Village: Recycled Rhetoric and Disposable People
Jan Knippers Black

Mainstreaming Microfinance:
How Lending to the Poor Began, Grew and Came of Age in Bolivia
Elisabeth Rhyne

New Roles and Relevance:
Development NGOs and the Challenge of Change
Edited by David Lewis and Tina Wallace

Patronage or Partnership: Local Capacity Building in Humanitarian Crises
Edited by Ian Smillie for the Humanitarianism and War Project

Reconcilable Differences: Turning Points in Ethnopolitical Conflict
Edited by Sean Byrne and Cynthia L. Irvin

Sustainable Livelihoods: Building on the Wealth of the Poor
Kristen Helmore and Naresh Singh

Transcending Neoliberalism: Community-Based Development in Latin America
Edited by Henry Veltmeyer and Anthony O'Malley

War's Offensive on Women:
The Humanitarian Challenge in Bosnia, Kosovo and Afghanistan
Julie A. Mertus for the Humanitarianism and War Project

Where Corruption Lives
Edited by Gerald E. Caiden, O.P. Dwivedi, Joseph Jabbra

Visit Kumarian Press at **www.kpbooks.com** or
call **toll-free 800.289.2664** for a complete catalog.

Kumarian Press, located in Bloomfield, Connecticut, is dedicated to publishing and distributing books and other media that will have a positive social and economic impact on the lives of peoples living in "Third World" conditions no matter where they live.